SLAVERY

AT MONTICELLO

SLAVERY
AT MONTICELLO

Lucia Stanton

Preface by Julian Bond

THOMAS JEFFERSON MEMORIAL FOUNDATION

Monticello Monograph Series

1996

The Thomas Jefferson Memorial Foundation, Inc.

This publication was made possible by a gift from Luella and Martin Davis.

The contents of this book originally appeared in *Jeffersonian Legacies,*
edited by Peter S. Onuf (Charlottesville: University Press of Virginia, 1993).
Permission to reprint is gratefully acknowledged by the
Thomas Jefferson Memorial Foundation.

Background cover photograph: Isaac Jefferson (1775–c1850), blacksmith,
tinsmith, and nailer at Monticello (Daguerrotype c1847, Tracy W. McGregor
Library, Special Collections Department, University of Virginia Library).

Designed by Gibson Parsons Design.
Printed by Spencer Printing, Richmond, Virginia.

ISBN 1-882886-02-X

PREFACE

ORE THAN ANYONE, Thomas Jefferson embodies the American conundrum on race. Author of the Declaration of Independence, he is best remembered for his advocacy of liberty. But freedom's advocate owned and sold slaves and trafficked in human beings; he grew to believe more and more in black inferiority. This gross imbalance he represents between national promise and execution remains our greatest state embarrassment today.

So central is he to American history and our view of ourselves as Americans that we cannot learn enough about him.

In today's culture, Jefferson is at once ambiguous and ubiquitous; he appears on a skit on the popular program 'Saturday Night Live' in 1992; a student asks then-Governor Bill Clinton—whose middle name is Jefferson—how the candidate differs from his namesake. The historian James McGregor Burns has a dog called 'Mr. Jefferson', not 'Tom'.

Writing about the 1995 movie 'Jefferson in Paris' *People* magazine says Jefferson has "preternatural versatility".[1]

No better example of that adaptability can be found than in a *Washington Post* story. The Jefferson quote fairly jumped off the page. The story was not about any of the themes we normally associate with Jefferson—great clashes between individual freedoms and larger social goals, religious freedoms, majority rule tempered by concerns for minority rights, representative government, or public education.

"Eternal vigilance, as our good friend Thomas Jefferson once noted" a partner in the law firm of Squire, Sanders and Dempsey wrote, "is not only the price of liberty, it is also the price of a clean and attractive office."[2]

That versatility also made him and his noblest words available to generations of fighters for human freedom; not at all unexpectedly, he remains available too for those who would deny and restrict freedom for others.

That early black anti-slavery opponents and past and present-day enemies of equality find him convenient ought not surpirse anyone. He warned his friends that "every word which goes from me, whether verbally or in writing, becomes the subject of so much malignant distortion and perverted construction that I am obliged to caution my friends …"[3]

His black contemporaries railed against the contradiction between his words and deeds.

After his death, and as Jefferson the man faded from memory, the man's most noble words achieved a life far beyond his person, constantly available to blacks who used them to try to pull the nation toward the goals Jefferson's words had pledged.

A black contemporary, District of Columbia surveyor Benjamin Banneker, wrote Jefferson that he had heard "that your sentiments are concurrent with mine, which are, that one universal Father hath given being to us all …. we are all in the same family and stand in the same relation to him."

Banneker quoted Jefferson's words from the Declaration back to him, and charged him with "detaining by fraud and violence so numerous a part of my brethren, under groaning captivity, and cruel oppression …."[4]

Following Jefferson's death in 1826, appeals to Jefferson the man ceased to be possible; appeals to Jefferson's ideals succeeded them. The protest literature of the 19th Century is filled with the Declaration's prelude as argument against slavery, and later, 20th Century freedom fighters used it to protest segregation and white oppression.

For most, the slave owner receded and the liberty lover took priority; even Dr. Martin Luther King embraced Jefferson to argue for equality.

For King, and others who summoned Jefferson in defense of liberty, the significant Jefferson was not the Secretary of State or President or author of the Virginia Statute on Religious Freedom, the farmer or slave holder; he was the author of the self-evident truths that all are equal.

Now Cinder Stanton shows us the Jefferson convenience forgot, and shows him to us in the home he built among the 'family'—slave and natural—he assembled around him.

This Jefferson is a much more complicated figure, but that complexity allows us a closer look at the inconsistency of the man and his age—and ours.

We also meet the black members of the Monticello family. Here they become real women and men, sons and daughters, wives and husbands, artisans and laborers and chefs, loyal to the master and run-aways—whole people with personalities and lives as private as being property would allow.

Their relationships with each other and with their owner illuminate his life and theirs and the disparity between the great work for which all remember him and his lifestyle on the mountain.

Jefferson remains a puzzle, but Stanton has given us a closer look than any previously available of Jefferson's relatiohship with his family.

His larger American family has much to learn from what we read here.

— JULIAN BOND

[1] *People* magazine, April 10, 1995.

[2] "Regs, Legs, Mugs and Rugs: The New Law Firm Order of Eating, Dressing and Decorating," by Linda Himelstein, *The Washington Post*, September 13, 1992, p. C-1.

[3] Philip S. Foner, *Basic Writings of Thomas Jefferson* (New York, 1944), p. 659.

[4] Benjamin Banneker, "Letter to Thomas Jefferson," *A Documentary History of the Negro People of the United States, Vol. 1*, ed. Herbert Aptheker (New York, 1969), pp. 23-26.

Lucy (1811–), daughter of Ben and Lilly, one of 130 slaves sold at auction at Monticello in January 1827 (Mason County Museum, Maysville, Kentucky).

Charlottesville Central Gazette, 13 Jan. 1827 (American Antiquarian Society).

EXECUTOR'S SALE.

Will be sold, on the fifteenth of January, at Monticello, in the county of Albemarle, the whole of the residue of the personal estate of Thomas Jefferson, dec., consisting of **130 VALUABLE NEGROES,** Stock, Crop, &c. Household and Kitchen Furniture. The attention of the public is earnestly invited to this property. The negroes are believed to be the most valuable for their number ever offered at one time in the State of Virginia. The household furniture, many valuable historical and portrait paintings, busts of marble and plaister of distinguished individuals; one of marble of Thomas Jefferson, by Caracci, with the pedestal and truncated column on which it stands; a polygraph or copying instrument used by Thomas Jefferson, for the last twenty-five years; with various other articles curious and useful to men of business and private families. The terms of sale will be accommodating and made known previous to the day. The sale will be continued from day to day until completed. This sale being unavoidable, it is a sufficient guarantee to the public, that it will take place at the time and place appointed.

THOMAS J. RANDOLPH,
Executor of Th: Jefferson, dec.

January 6, 1827—2t

The paintings and busts of Thos. Jefferson, dec. will not be offered for sale on the 15th of January next; but will be sent to some one of the large cities and then sold, after due notice.

To give liberty to, or rather, to abandon persons whose habits have been formed in slavery is like abandoning children.[1]

O N JANUARY 15, 1827, Monticello blacksmith Joseph Fossett may have left his anvil to watch the bidding begin. His wife Edith and their eight children were among the "130 valuable negroes" offered in the executor's sale of the estate of Thomas Jefferson. "The negroes are believed to be the most valuable for their number ever offered at one time in the State of Virginia," declared the advertisement placed by Thomas Jefferson Randolph, Jefferson's grandson and executor. Despite bitterly cold weather, a large crowd assembled for the five-day sale, and bidding was brisk. Surprising sums were paid for faded prints and old-fashioned tables, while the slaves brought prices averaging 70 percent more than their appraised values.[2]

By the terms of Jefferson's will, Fossett would become a free man in July. Now, his wife, two infant sons, and two teenaged daughters were sold to three different bidders for a total of $1,350. "Thank heaven the whole of this dreadful business is over," wrote Jefferson's granddaughter on January 25, "and has been attended with as few distressing occurrences as the case would admit." Her brother remembered that week over forty years later as "a sad scene" and likened it to "a captured village in ancient times when all were sold as slaves."[3]

The monumental debt kept in check by Jefferson's presence overwhelmed all the residents of Monticello, both black and white. In the three years after his death the black families were dispersed by sale and the white family left the mountaintop and put the house on the market. The plantation "family" that Jefferson had nurtured and controlled for sixty years was no more. In the end, he had abandoned his "children."

I give a gold watch to each of my grand children, who shall not have already recieved one from me, to be purchased and delivered by my executor, to my grandsons at the age of 21. and grand-daughters at that of sixteen.

I give to my good, affectionate, and faithful servant Burwell his freedom, and the sum of three hundred Dollars to buy necessaries to commence his trade of painter and glazier, or to use otherwise as he pleases. I give also to my good servants John Hemings and Joe Fosset their freedom at the end of one year after my death: and to each of them respectively all the tools of their respective shops or callings: and it is my will that a comfortable log-house be built for each of the three servants so emancipated on some part of my lands convenient to them with respect to the residence of their wives, and to Charlottesville and the University, where they will be mostly employed, and reasonably convenient also to the interests of the proprietor of the lands; of which houses I give the use of one, with a curtilage of an acre to each, during his life or personal occupation thereof.

I give also to John Hemings the service of his two apprentices, Madison and Eston, Hemings until their respective ages of twenty one years, at which period respectively, I give them their freedom. and I humbly and earnestly request of the legislature of Virginia a confirmation of the bequest of freedom to these servants, with permission to remain in this state where their families and connections are, as an additional instance of the favor, of which I have recieved so many other manifestations, in the course of my life, and for which I now give them my last, solemn, and dutiful thanks.

In testimony that this is a Codicil to my will of yesterday's date, and that it is to modify so far the provisions of that will, I have written it all with my own hand, on two pages, to each of which I subscribe my name this 17th day of March one thousand eight hundred and twenty six.

Th: Jefferson

Codicil of Jefferson's will, 17 March 1826 (Special Collections Department, University of Virginia Library, on deposit from Albemarle County Circuit Court).

"My Family"

In 1776 Jefferson made a census of the "Number of souls in my family."[4] His Albemarle County "family" numbered 117, including, besides his wife and daughter, 16 free men (his overseers and hired workmen), their wives and children, and 83 slaves. Throughout his life Jefferson used the word "family" for both a group of people connected by blood and—according to more ancient usage—all those under a head of household, or, in his case, plantation owner. In 1801 he vaccinated "70 or 80 of my own family" against smallpox; in 1819 he spoke of the voracious appetite for pork of "our enormously large family." At times this usage required the addition of qualifying adjectives. Jefferson wrote

Number of souls in my family in Albemarle as given in this year.	Free	Slaves
Males of 16 years old & upwds	17	22.
Females of 16 years old & upwds	5	17
Males below 16.	4	22
Females below 16.	8	22
Number of Free & slaves	34	83
Number in the whole		117.

Jefferson's 1776 census of the Monticello "family" (Farm Book; courtesy of the Massachusetts Historical Society).

that his son-in-law's "white family" had recovered from a prevailing illness in 1806, and, in 1815, he noted the surprising number of sick "in our family, both in doors and out"—making a neat spatial distinction between the Jefferson-Randolph family inside the Monticello house and the black men, women, and children living in cabins on the mountaintop and adjacent farms.[5]

Joseph Fossett joined this family in November 1780, born to Mary Hemings (b. 1753) and an unknown father. She was the oldest child of Elizabeth (Betty) Hemings (c1735-1807), who, with her ten children, became Jefferson's property on January 14, 1774, on the division of the estate of his father-in-law John Wayles.[6] On that date Jefferson acquired 135 slaves who, added to the 52 slaves derived from his inheritance from his father, made him the second largest slaveholder in Albemarle County. Thereafter, the number of slaves he owned fluctuated above and below the figure of two hundred—with increases through births offset by periodic sales that were part of an attempt to pay off the almost £4,000 debt that accompanied the Wayles inheritance. Between 1784 and 1794 Jefferson disposed of 161 people by sale or gift.[7]

Unlike his father-in-law, Jefferson never engaged in the commercial buying and selling of humans. His infrequent purchases were usually made to fulfill needs of the moment and selling was primarily a reluctant reaction to financial demands. As Jefferson wrote in 1820, he had "scruples about selling negroes but for delinquency, or on their own request."[8] Several known transactions were intended to unite families. The purchase of Ursula in 1773 involved buying her husband Great George from a second owner. In 1805, Jefferson "reluctantly" sold Brown, a twenty-year-old nailer, to unite him with his wife, the slave of a brickmason about to leave Monticello. On this occasion Jefferson declared himself "always willing to indulge connections seriously formed by those people, where it can be done reasonably."[9]

In 1807 Jefferson bought the wife of his blacksmith Moses when her owner emigrated to Kentucky. "Nobody feels more strongly than I do," he wrote at the time, "the desire to make all practicable sacrifices to keep man and wife together who have imprudently married out of their respective families." This final phrase, a telling indication of the dual nature of Jefferson's recognition of the importance of the black family, reveals his hope that his slaves would seek spouses only within their master's domain. "There is nothing I desire so much as that all the young people in the estate should intermarry with one another and stay at home," Jefferson wrote his Poplar Forest overseer. "They are worth a great deal more in that case than when they have husbands and wives abroad." His methods for discouraging romance beyond the plantation boundaries are not known, but he did use rewards to encourage "prudent" courtship. To the slave women, for instance, he promised an extra pot and crocus bed "when they take husbands at home."[10]

Jefferson realized the potency of family bonds for the African-American members of his extended household. In 1814, there is even a note of envy in his comparison of the lot of English laborers and American slaves. Slaves "have the comfort, too, of numerous families, in the midst of whom they live without want, or fear of it." This "comfort" was not always possible for whites. Jefferson all his life sought to draw to the neighborhood of Monticello both kin and kindred spirits, but with only limited success. The mobility of white Virginians separated parent from child and sibling from sibling. His sister emigrated with her husband to Kentucky and his younger daughter's husband could not be persuaded to leave his Tidewater planta-

1774. Location of Slaves. for 1774. 15

Monticello.

+ Martin. 1755.	* Goliah.
Bob. 1762	* Hercules.
Jamey 1765	* Gill. died. 1774.
+ Mary. 1753.	* Fanny
+ Bett 1759.	Suckey. 1765.
Scilla. 1762.	Frankey. 1767.
+ Old Jenny.	Gill. 1769.
+ Ned. 1760.	* Quash.
+ George	* Nell.
+ Ursula.	* Bella. 1757.
George. 1759.	* Charles. 1760.
Bagwell. 1768.	Jenny. 1768.
Archy. 1773. died. July 1774.	* Betty.
— Juno	* Toby. junr. 1753.
— Luna 1758.	* Cate.
+ Dinah. 1761.	Hanah. Jan. 1770.
+ Jupiter 1743.	Rachael. Oct. 1773.
+ Suck 1758.	
+ Frank 1757.	
+ Barnaby 1760.	
+ Sanco. } sold.	
+ Abram } Carpenters.	
+ Bob. 1757 } sold Jan. 1782.	
+ Lewis	
+ Jame Hubbard	
+ York	
+ Peter } Watermen.	
+ King	

Jefferson's Farm Book, 1774 (courtesy of the Massachusetts Historical Society).

Negroes alienated from 1784. to 1794. inclusive.

Sale at Elkhill. 1785. Jan. 31.		Marriage settlement to Randolph	Sale in Bedford. Dec. 1791.
Stephen. Tho.ᵉ Norris.	130-0-0	1790.	Tom.
Sall		Billy.	Mima
John } James Foster	131-10-0	Sarah	Armistead
aggy. John Austin	117-0-0	Peg.	Polly
Tomo. Richard James	50-0-0	Lewis	Nat } Solomon } Danl. B. Perrow 183-0-0
Dilcey. Joseph Ashley.	122-10-0	Abby.	Will.
Harry. Thomas Randolph.	105-0-0	Patty	Bella
Peter.		Harry.	Charles
Hanah		Jack.	Jesse
Betty		Patty Kennon.	Jenny. } John Christian 198-10-0
Sal.		Betty	Billy. Joseph Dickinson 56-0-0
George		Judy	a lame boy 30-10-0
Cuffy } Vincent Markham 385-0-0		Tom.	Ned
Billy Warry. Philip Gooch.	137-10-0	Lucy.	Phoebe
Nat. James Carter	136-10-0	Polly	Joe
Daniel. George Saunders.	72-0-0	Davy.	Isabel
Philip. Miles Selden.	135-0-0	Jeffrey.	Frank } William Harris 187-0-0
Judy		Joan.	Annaky. Reuben Smith. 90-10-0
Dinah. } Tandy Rice.	130-0-0	Scilla.	Charles
Sue		Nancy	Betty
Glester.		Lundy	Peter. } John Depriest 108-10-0
Sall } Robt. Coleman.	126-10-0	Betty	Rachael 80-0-0
Ambrose		Jupiter	Peter.
Hanah		Phyllis	Suckey
Nanny		Phyllis	Lucy. } John Bolling 160-0-0
Ambrose		Sandy.	old Lucy. Robert Hawkins 43-5-0
Abram		John	Milly. Wm. Philips 75-0-0
Abby.		Sam. 27	Sam. George Reaveley. 42-10-0
Sally } Saml. Woodson. 420-0-0		given to R. etux. by deed	Beck. Do. 78-10-0 29. 1302-15-0
Sanco.		1790 Nov. 6.	Sale in Bedford. Dec. 14. 1792
Nanny } Wm. Richardson. 126-10-0		Suck.	Will. Danl. B. Perrow 41-0-0
31. 2325-0-0		Philip Evans.	Judy } James Branch. 81-5-0 amy
Valuation to Hastings Marks.		Scilla.	Frank. John Clarke 111-10-0
Gill. born 69. 72-10-0		Suckey.	Sam
Suckey. 57-10-0		Johnny.	Dilcey
Nance. 61.		Mingo.	Ambrose
Billy. 80.		George	Hannah
Critta. } 95-0-0		Molly. 8.	Dinah } Joshua Early. 242-15-0
Cyrus. 72. 47-10-0		marriage settlement to J.W. Eppes. Oct. 97	York. Robt. Hawkins 53-0-0
Charlotte. 68. } 67-10-0		Isaac.	James. 30-12-0
a suckl. child)		Iris.	11. 560.2-
Daniel. 72. 47-10-0		Squire	
Betty. 42-10-0		Joice	Albemarle. Jan. 15. 1793.
10 230-0-0		Lucinda	Dinah
		Sarah	Sally.
Frankey. 67. Dr. Gilmer.		Saney	Lizzy } Kinsolving 139-15-0
		Squy }	1792. Sep. 20.
		Daniel	Mary
		Judy Hix	Bob.
		Jim	Sally } Thomas Bell. 115-0-0
		Austin	1794. Sep. 19.
		York	Theria.
		Phelps	Mary
		Thamar.	Lucy
		Rachael	Betsy
		Lucy	Susan
		Scilla	Sally } James Monroe. 173-0-0
		Nelly	Dec. 24. Bob. 60-0-0
		Letty	
		Phyllis	
		Sophia	
		Sally	
		Clarinda	
		Goliah.	
		Val	
		Martin	
		Lucy	
		Nathan	
		Linda 31.	

Jefferson's list of slaves sold or given away between 1784 and 1794 (Sol Feinstone Collection, David Library of the American Revolution, on deposit at the American Philosophical Society).

tion. Jefferson's fatherly tenacity kept his elder daughter Martha always at or near Monticello, at considerable jeopardy to her marriage.

His rosy picture of the "comfort of numerous families" was drawn at a time when Virginian society was progressively destabilized by westward migration. He must, therefore, have witnessed how frequently the ties within extended slave families were severed, and he would have heard constant expression of the "dread of separation" that Frederick Douglass called the "most painful to the majority of slaves."[11]

Jefferson's awareness of the slave's attachment to a particular spot on earth and the extended network of relations that lived on it played a significant part in his actions as a slaveholder. He could foster family ties through benevolent intercession, he could exploit them to control behavior, or ignore them in the interests of efficient management. These ties could even inhibit his actions toward improving the lot of his slaves through emancipation or removal to cotton country, where conditions were considered more favorable to their wellbeing. Even freedom was not, in Jefferson's mind, sufficient justification for uprooting whole families. In 1814, he wrote that "the laws do not permit us to turn them loose," evidently referring to the 1806 act declaring that freed slaves must leave the state within a year. When his son-in-law Thomas Mann Randolph launched a scheme in 1802 to take his slaves to "a mild climate and gentle labor" in Georgia, Jefferson did consider sending "such of my negroes as could be persuaded to it." But in 1822, Martha Randolph knew her father "would never listen … for a moment" to the family's latest plan to try their fortunes further south—"although moving [his slaves] in a body would occasion little or no distress to them."[12]

Slaves were both humans and property, and as the protector of a large household and the manager of a working plantation Jefferson always had to play two roles. He was gratified when "moral as well as interested considerations" were in accord, as when prescribing lighter labors for women with infant children in 1819: "I consider the labor of a breeding woman as no object, and that a child raised every 2. years is of more profit than the crop of the best laboring man. In this, as in all other cases, providence has made our interest and our duties coincide perfectly." But he must have had daily reminders of the frequent contradiction between "interest" and "duty."[13]

In his role as plantation manager, Jefferson's efforts to maximize the utility of each man, woman, and child led to regular interference in the family lives of his slaves. The demands of productivity limited his respect for the integrity of the black family. Like many other enlightened Virginians, Jefferson always specified that slaves be sold in family units: husbands were not separated from wives, nor parents from young children. But once black boys or girls reached the age of ten or twelve and their working lives began, they lost their status as children and, with it, the guarantee of family stability. Teenagers were often separated from their families through sale or transfer to other plantations. Four boys from Poplar Forest, aged ten to twelve, were sent to Monticello to work in the nailery in the 1790s, and in 1813 two fourteen-year-old girls left Bedford County to learn weaving and spinning in the Albemarle County textile factory. The privileged household servants were particularly vulnerable to teenage separation, as their young masters or mistresses grew up and married. Betty Brown left her family to attend the newly married Martha Jefferson at age thirteen, and her niece, Betsy Hemings, was fourteen when she was given to Jefferson's daughter Maria on her marriage in 1797.[14]

Dinah was sold in 1792 with "her younger children" to accomplish the double objective of paying off a debt and uniting her with her husband. When Jefferson purchased the weaver Nance Hemings from his sister, he listened to a mother's plea. Nance "wishes me to buy her children," he wrote, "but I would not purchase the boy; as to the youngest child, if she insists on it, and my sister desires it, I would take it." Fifteen-year-old Billy was left in Louisa County and twelve-year-old Critta only came to Albemarle because she was bought by Jefferson's son-in-law.[15]

Joe Fossett was also separated from his mother by sale. During Jefferson's five-year absence in France, Mary Hemings was hired out to Thomas Bell, a respected Charlottesville merchant. In 1792 she asked to be sold to Bell, the father of her two youngest children, Robert Washington and Sally Jefferson. Jefferson asked his superintendent to "dispose of Mary according to her desire, with such of her younger children as she chose." Bob and Sally remained with their mother and became Bells, and eleven-year-old Joe and nine-year-old Betsy were now on their own at Monticello.[16]

Joe spent his days in and around the Monticello house, one of nine house ser-

Jefferson's list of clothing for household slaves (Farm Book; courtesy of the Massachusetts Historical Society).

vants. He and three of his cousins were the fetchers and carriers, the fire builders, the table setters and waiters; they met guests at the east portico and ventured forth on errands. They were the "boys" that Martha Jefferson Randolph finally got "in tolerable order" during Jefferson's absence, after some accidents to the household china.[17]

In the house Joe was surrounded by members of his own family, all Hemingses. The household staff included his uncles James and Peter, his aunts Sally and Critta, his cousins Wormley, Burwell, and Brown, and his sister Betsy.[18] From their arrival at Monticello as part of the Wayles estate in 1774, the children of Betty Hemings had assumed the primary roles in the Monticello household. Robert Hemings (1762-1819) replaced Jupiter as Jefferson's valet and travelling attendant; Martin Hemings (b. 1755) became the butler; Betty Hemings and her daughters were employed in cleaning, sewing, and in personal attendance on Martha Jefferson and her children. In the period of Jefferson's retirement to Monticello from 1794 to 1797, visitors who did not wander over to Mulberry Row or down to the cellar dependencies would have seen only Hemingses.

Jefferson's grandson Thomas Jefferson Randolph recalled a slightly later period, when the "entire household of servants with the exception of an under cook and carriage driver consisted of one family connection and their wives …. It was a source of bitter jealousy to the other slaves, who liked to account for it with other reasons than the true one; viz. superior intelligence, capacity and fidelity to trusts." Monticello overseer Edmund Bacon spoke of the women of the household: "They were old family servants and great favorites …. I was instructed to take no control of them." And more than one visitor would have noted, as did the Duc de La Rochefoucauld-Liancourt in 1796, that the slaves visible at Monticello were remarkably light-skinned. "I have even seen," he wrote at a time when Sally Hemings's children were not yet on the scene, "and particularly at Mr. Jefferson's, slaves who have neither in their color nor features a single trace of their origin, but they are sons of slave mothers and consequently slaves."[19]

Edmund Bacon (1785–1866), Monticello overseer 1806 to 1822 (courtesy of Mrs. Frank Coscia).

According to her grandson, Betty Hemings was the daughter of an African slave and an English sea captain, and at least seven of her children had white fathers. Isaac Jefferson (1775–c1850), former Monticello slave whose reminiscences were recorded in 1847, recalled that Betty's children Robert and James Hemings were "bright mulattoes" and Sally was "mighty near white."[20] Many of the third generation of Hemingses were even lighter. Without reviving the debate over the paternity of Sally Hemings's children, it is sufficient to note here that several and perhaps all of Betty Hemings's daughters formed relationships with white men.[21] In at least one case, that of Sally Hemings, the children had seven-eighths white ancestry and thus were white by Virginia law, which declared that a person "who shall have one fourth part or more of negro blood, shall … be deemed a mulatto."

Jefferson looked up this statute in 1815 and, after demonstrating its effects in a series of algebraic formulas, stated that "our Canon considers 2. crosses with the pure white, and a 3d. with any degree of mixture, however small, as clearing the issue of the negro blood." "But observe," he continued, "that this does not reestablish freedom, which depends on the condition of the mother." If the issue of the third cross were emancipated, "he becomes a free *white* man, and a citizen of the US. to all intents and purposes."[22] Thus, future citizens of the United States were being held in bondage at Monticello.

Jefferson did free all of Sally Hemings's children. He allowed Harriet and Beverly to "run away," providing Harriet money and stage fare to Philadelphia, and gave Madison and Eston Hemings their freedom in his will. Overseer Edmund Bacon remembered Harriet's departure, when "people said he freed her because she was his own daughter" (Bacon's own candidate for paternity was deleted in the published version of his reminiscences), but the reasons given by Jefferson's granddaughter Ellen Randolph Coolidge accord with his racial formulas. In 1858 she stated that it was her grandfather's principle to "allow such of his slaves as were sufficiently white to pass for white men, to withdraw from the plantation; it was called running away, but they were never reclaimed."[23]

"It is almost impossible for slaves to give a correct account of their male parentage," wrote former slave Henry Bibb in 1849. The fathers of Betty Hemings's children and grandchildren can never be positively identified. The only certainty is

Jefferson noted the running away in 1822 of Beverly and Harriet Hemings in his "Roll of the negroes according to their ages" (Farm Book; courtesy of the Massachusetts Historical Society).

that some of them were white men, and those implicated by their contemporaries ranged from overseers and hired artisans to sprigs of the local aristocracy, family kinsmen, and even the master himself.[24] Jefferson, thus, who often stated his "aversion" to racial mixture, lived surrounded by its examples.[25]

Little is known about miscegenation at Monticello beyond the Hemings family. The presence of two mulattoes in the legacy of Peter Jefferson suggests that the crossing of racial lines was nothing new on the mountain.[26] Nevertheless, the Hemings family—as Thomas Jefferson Randolph's statement indicated—seems to have been a caste apart.

All the slaves freed by Jefferson in his lifetime or in his will were members of this family. Two, Robert and Martin, were allowed a measure of mobility no other slave had—they often hired themselves out to other masters during Jefferson's long absences in public service. Only Betty Hemings and her daughters were spared the grueling weeks of the wheat harvest, when every healthy slave was drafted to bring in the crop. None of her twelve children, and only two of her more than twenty grandchildren found spouses "at home." One of the latter, Burwell Colbert, even married his own first cousin. Known husbands were drawn from the local community, both free black and white, and wives from the household staffs of neighboring plantations.[27] Only Joe Fossett and Wormley Hughes, who married a niece of Isaac Jefferson, found wives at Monticello.

At the boundary between the black and white worlds at Monticello, the Hemings family has occupied the foreground of all accounts of the slave community there because we know more about them. Their domination of the documentary record derives from the positions they occupied in the household and Mulberry Row shops, under perpetual observation by their master and his family.

"To Labor for Another"[28]

In 1794 Joe Fossett's life took on a new dimension. He was one of "a dozen little boys from 10. to 16. years of age" whom Jefferson installed in a new nailery on Mulberry Row.[29] Retired to Monticello, Jefferson devoted most of his energies at this time to the reformation of his farms, impoverished by thirty years of the extractive rotation of corn and tobacco and the unsupervised management of stewards and overseers. Expecting the change from tobacco to wheat production and the inaugu-ration of his complex crop rotation schemes to cause a temporary decrease in farm production, he had determined to find a new source of income. He chose the pro-duction of nails, because it required little capital outlay and was within the capacities of his own slave labor force.

In the first three years of the nailery's operation, Jefferson was a daily pres-ence. His surviving accounts reveal that he must have risen at dawn to weigh out the nailrod given to the nailers and returned toward dusk to weigh the nails they pro-duced. An "Estimate on the actual work of the autumn of 1794" summarizes the results of his daily balancing of the scales. "Moses wastes 15 lb. in the [hundred-weight]," he began, writing down the name of each nailer and the average amount of iron he wasted in the nailmaking process. Fourteen-year-old Joe Fossett was one of the most efficient, wasting only nineteen pounds of iron per hundredweight, while two ten-year-olds—Burwell and James—were predictably the least efficient, making only seventy-one pounds of nails from every hundred pounds of nailrod. Another ten-year-old, however, the future wagoner Davy, was the third of nine in efficiency.[30]

Here was a new scene for Joe, Wormley, and Burwell, who now divided their time between the Monticello house and the Mulberry Row nailery, where a dozen teenagers stood at their anvils around four fires, pointing and heading nails with heavy hammers until they had completed their appointed tasks. Because of his household duties Joe's daily task was about two-thirds that of the fulltime nailers—250 to 350 nails depending on size. Two years later, when he left the house to pursue the ironworking trade fulltime, his task was increased. One page of accounts shows Jefferson apparently calculating the average production of his nailers in order to set a new and higher daily task. In an analysis Jefferson made in April 1796, Joe Fossett was the third most profitable nailer, making 316 pounds of nails in three months and earning for his master an average daily profit of about sixty cents.[31]

The Mulberry Row nailery served as more than a new source of income. It allowed Jefferson to observe the abilities and attitudes of his young male slaves and to select their future careers. By the same token, in the nailery these young men had a chance to influence their future by their own actions. Many of them evidently chose to please their master by their performance and eventually occupied the most important artisan and household positions on the mountain. Several became blacksmiths, carpenters, and coopers; one became the head gardener and another the Monticello butler; a few were unable to avert the usual fate of farm labor; and at least one, James Hubbard—the most "wasteful" in 1794, chose the route of resistance.

The nailery was also an important part of Jefferson's perpetual effort to make the most efficient use of his labor force. His constant attempts to eliminate every pocket of idleness from his operation went beyond the ordinary profitseeking of plantation managers. Neither youth, age, illness, nor weather were allowed to stop the plantation machine. There is even a note of pride in Jefferson's accounts of his successful efforts to provide for all his wants by harnessing the energies of children. In the summer of 1795 he wrote that "a nailery which I have established with my own negro boys now provides completely for the maintenance of my family." A few months earlier he had declared that "my new trade of nail-making is to me in this country what an additional title of nobility or the ensigns of a new order are in Europe."[32]

A detail of Jefferson's 1796 nailery accounts, with his "Analysis of work" calibrating the profitability of the nailers (William Andrews Clark Memorial Library, University of California, Los Angeles).

Twenty years later Jefferson's favorite project was the textile factory, which "only employs a few women, children and invalids who could do little in the farm." Appropriate tasks were found for slaves past the age for farm labor. "The negroes too old to be hired," Jefferson wrote his steward in 1788, "could they not make a good profit by cultivating cotton?" Some older women served as nurses or cooks in the quarters while others joined the older men on the vegetable gardening team, dubbed by Jefferson the "veteran aids" and "senile corps."[33]

The sick who were not bedridden were treated with gentle doses of alternative labor. When all hands were diverted to the digging of a canal in 1793, the "inva-lids" were to "work only when they shall be able. They will probably be equal to the hauling away the earth and forming it into a bank on the side next the river." Poplar Forest's former "head man" Nace was to be "entirely kept from labour until he recov-ers." Jefferson suggested, nevertheless, that he spend his days indoors, shelling corn or making shoes or baskets.[34]

So that neither climate nor circumstance could interrupt the hum of activity on his plantation, Jefferson gave his laborers a variety of skills. Barnaby and Shep-herd, whose main trade was carpentry, were to join Phil when he "proceeds to the making shoes for the people … in order to perfect themselves in shoemaking." Car-penters and coopers were also charcoalburners. Nailers were dispatched to the woods with axes when there was an immediate need for clearing land. Poplar Forest blacksmiths, when there was no work, could fell wood for charcoal or work in the fields; Bess made butter "during the season" and worked in the spinning house when there was no dairy work.[35]

Male domestic servants, in particular, were trained in a trade they could pur-sue during Jefferson's long absences in public service. Jupiter was a stonecutter as well as manservant and groom. Burwell Colbert, butler at Monticello for many years, was a skilled glazier and painter. Israel Gillett, a waiter and postillion, worked as a carder in the textile shop when his services were not needed by the household and, as already mentioned, the young boys in the house filled their extra hours with nailmaking. Although overseer Edmund Bacon wrote that the female house ser-vants had "very little to do" when Jefferson was absent in Washington, later refer-ences reveal that some were expected to master textile skills and complete a daily carding or spinning task.[36]

Joe Fossett's own training probably began in earnest in 1796. In his Farm Book Jefferson had penned a script for the childhood of his slaves: "Children till 10. years to serve as nurses. From 10. to 16. the boys make nails, the girls spin. At 16. go into the ground or learn trades." In 1796 Fossett—now sixteen—was issued overalls instead of his usual house servants' clothing allowance, and for several years he di-vided his time between nailmaking—becoming a foreman of nailers—and learning the blacksmithing trade. He first worked under Isaac Jefferson's brother Little

Jefferson's prescription for the working lives of the slave children (Farm Book; courtesy of the Massachusetts Historical Society).

George and in 1801 began his training under a remarkable new teacher, William Stewart. Jefferson had found "the best workman in America, but the most eccentric one" in Philadelphia and employed him for six years—"several years longer than he would otherwise have done," wrote Edmund Bacon, "in order that his own servants might learn his trade thoroughly." Drink was Stewart's downfall and, when he got into "his idle frolics," Joe Fossett had to carry forward the work of the blacksmith shop on his own. When Jefferson's patience ran out at the end of 1807, Stewart was dismissed and Fossett became the head blacksmith, running the shop until Jefferson's death. Bacon described Fossett as "a very fine workman; could do anything it was necessary to do with steel or iron."[37]

The workmen hired to build and rebuild the Monticello house also imparted their considerable skills to their African-American assistants. Jefferson had friends in Europe and Philadelphia on the lookout for the best masons and woodworkers. Moses was to be the "disciple" of a stonemason expected from Scotland. John Hemings worked first with David Watson, who had deserted from the British army in the Revolution, and then with a newly arrived Irishman, James Dinsmore. Together Hemings and Dinsmore crafted Monticello's beautiful interior woodwork, to which, in Jefferson's opinion, "there is nothing superior in the US." Hemings alone was responsible for the interior joinery work at Poplar Forest and he reigned in the Monticello woodworking shop for all the years of Jefferson's retirement.[38]

"To be independent for the comforts of life," wrote Jefferson in 1816, "we must fabricate them ourselves."[39] To enable his own slave laborers to produce both the necessities and some of the comforts of life, he imported to Monticello at various times a Scottish gardener, an English brewer, a German painter, and a French chef.

He hired white masons, smiths, carriagebuilders, charcoalburners, and weavers for the time required to pass their skills to men and women who practiced their craft and in turn passed it on to others.

As an observant Madison Hemings remembered in 1873, Jefferson in the years of his retirement had "but little taste or care for agricultural pursuits .... It was his mechanics he seemed mostly to direct, and in their operations he took great interest." Jefferson was certainly most comfortable in the management of his artisans, with whom his methods of personal control and rational incentives to industry were so successful. His daily supervising presence in the nailery in its first three years made it both profitable and relatively tranquil. A sense of pride and esprit de corps was instilled through rewards and special rations. Isaac Jefferson remembered that Jefferson "gave the boys in the nail factory a pound of meat a week, a dozen herrings, a quart of molasses, and peck of meal. Give them that wukked the best a suit of red or blue; encouraged them mightily." The special clothing prize would have had particular appeal in a community that received the equivalent of uniforms twice a year, and the Farm Book confirms a larger meat ration.[40]

Financial incentives were reserved for adult laborers. The blacksmith Little George, manager of the nailery, received a percentage of its profits. The Monticello coopers were allowed to sell for their own benefit every thirty-third flour barrel they made. Jefferson gave his slave charcoalburners a premium for efficiency, not just productivity. He paid them according to the average number of bushels of charcoal they could extract per cord of wood.[41] John Hemings the joiner and Burwell Colbert, butler and painter, were given an annual "gratuity" or "donation" of fifteen or twenty dollars—equivalent to one month's wages of a free workman.[42]

Joe Fossett and other artisans at Monticello carried on their work with a notable freedom from supervision. In 1798 Thomas Mann Randolph wrote an absent Jefferson about the slave manager of the nailery: "George I am sure could not stoop to my authority and I hope and believe he pushes your interests as well as I could." Jefferson was willing to give his tradesmen a remarkable measure of independence. On his departure from Monticello at the end of 1797, he left written instructions with his carpenters, merely asking his son-in-law to keep them "to their metal" by occasional questioning "as to their progress." A few years later he directed that

Wormley Hughes and Joe Fossett work on their own, with auger and gunpowder, blasting rock in the canal. Overseer Gabriel Lilly, however, could not bring himself to let them do this dangerous work out of his sight. Randolph, too, had doubts about Jefferson's wisdom in leaving his artisans "under no command." He was convinced they would become "idle and dissipated," but admitted Jefferson's confidence was "less abused than I expected" and "it confirms them in honesty."[43]

The power of Jefferson's personal control is apparent in an incident related by Edmund Bacon. About 1807 one of the nailers was discovered in the theft of several hundred pounds of nails. Brought before Jefferson, "he was mortified and distressed beyond measure. He had been brought up in the shop, and we all had confidence in him. Now his character was gone." Jefferson considered his shame sufficient punishment and, despite the expectations of the nailery manager, ordered no whipping. According to Bacon, the chastened offender found religion through this experience and was baptised soon afterwards.[44]

After Jefferson's return to public life, nailery profits shrank as cheaper British nails came on the market and the cooped-up crowd of teenagers became unruly. William Stewart, the blacksmith from the north, was entirely unequal to their management. In Jefferson's opinion, "they require a rigour of discipline to make them do reasonable work, to which he cannot bring himself." Overseer Gabriel Lilly began to resort to the whip and had to be restrained. Jefferson wrote that "it would destroy their value, in my estimation, to degrade them in their own eyes by the whip. This, therefore, must not be resorted to but in extremities; as they will be again under my government, I would chuse they should retain the stimulus of character."[45]

"I love industry and abhor severity," Jefferson wrote in 1805, and no reliable document portrays him in the act of applying physical correction.[46] Overseer Edmund Bacon recalled that Jefferson "was always very kind and indulgent to his servants. He would not allow them to be at all overworked, and he would hardly ever allow one of them to be whipped …. He could not bear to have a servant whipped, no odds how much he deserved it." His intercession in the affair of the nail thief was only one of a number of such incidents. In the case of Hercules, a runaway from Poplar Forest, Jefferson suggested to his overseer that, as "it is his first folly in this way," further punishment was inappropriate; his imprisonment in

Buckingham County jail had been sufficient. Another Poplar Forest slave, Phil Hubbard, was not to be punished for running away to Monticello: "Altho I had let them all know that their runnings away should be punished, yet Phill's character is not that of a runaway. I have known him from a boy and that he has not come off to sculk from his work."[47]

In Hercules's case, Jefferson advised the overseer to let him "recieve the pardon as from yourself alone, and not by my interference, for this is what I would have none of them to suppose." And he gave Thrimston, whose transgression is not specified, "a proper reprimand for his conduct," and assured him that punishment for any further misbehavior would be left to the discretion of the stonecutter for whom he worked.[48] Despite Jefferson's wish to remain hidden behind the cloak of his overseers' authority, it is apparent that first-time offenders, especially, turned to him frequently in expectation of leniency.

Jefferson's views on physical punishment no doubt reduced whipping on his plantations to levels well below those of many of his neighbors. The whip was, however, by no means eliminated. From the 1780s Jefferson employed on the Monticello plantation over twenty overseers with diverse temperaments and management styles.[49] Some were cruel, even by the standards of the day. William Page, "peevish and too ready to strike," spent four years in Jefferson's employ. When he later became overseer at John Wayles Eppes's neighboring Pantops, Eppes was unable to hire slaves in the neighborhood because of "the terror of Pages name." The "tyrannical" William McGehee, overseer at the Tufton farm for two years, carried a gun "for fear of an attack from the negroes." One of Monticello's white housejoiners deplored the cruelty of Gabriel Lilly, overseer there from 1801 to 1805. Lilly whipped Critta Hemings's seventeen-year-old son James three times in one day, when he was too ill to "raise his hand to his Head." Yet Jefferson considered it impossible to find "a man who fulfills my purposes better than" Lilly and would have kept him longer had he not demanded a doubling of his salary.[50]

The whippings that Jefferson himself ordered were mainly for the benefit of their witnesses. He had the chronic runaway Jame Hubbard brought to Monticello in irons and "severely flogged in the presence of his old companions."[51] And when the excuses of youth, sentiment, or special circumstances had been exhausted,

Jefferson invariably rid himself of disruptive elements by sale. Overseer Bacon remembered his orders: "If there was any servant that could not be got along without the chastising that was customary, to dispose of him."[52]

In 1803 an unforgettable example was made of an eighteen-year-old nailer. The usual turbulence of the nailery boiled over into violence in May, when Cary nearly killed Joe Fossett's cousin Brown with his hammer. Jefferson wrote home from Washington: "Should Brown recover so that the law shall inflict no punishment on Cary, it will be necessary for me to make an example of him in terrorem to others, in order to maintain the police so rigorously necessary among the nailboys." He was to be sold either to "negro purchasers from Georgia" or "in any other quarter so distant as never more to be heard of among us." It would seem to Cary's companions "as if he were put out of the way by death." In the language of this letter, Jefferson became increasingly vehement in his determination to deliver a shock to the family sensibilities of the African-Americans who would continue to share his mountaintop. He continued: "I should regard price but little in comparison with so distant an exile of him as to cut him off compleatly from ever again being heard of."[53]

By all accounts Jefferson was remarkably successful in surrounding himself with artisans and house servants of the proper "character," who united industry with trust. Jupiter and other "trusty servants" traveled alone all over Virginia, carrying large sums of money. In 1811 Jefferson promised "a trusty negro of my own" a reward in exchange for information on the whereabouts of a runaway.[54] Whereas George Washington's letters abound with exasperation at the performance of his craftsmen, Jefferson's are surprisingly silent on this head. Since it is doubtful that his expectations were lower, this suggests both the talents of his tradesmen and the success of his management methods.

With his farm laborers, however, Jefferson was less successful. He was always wrestling with the overseer problem. As his son-in-law expressed it, an overseer "will either reject all restraint or use it as an excuse for making no profit." Jefferson stated the case in the usual two parts in 1792, when he was contemplating a novel solution: "My first wish is that the labourers may be well treated, the second that they may enable me to have that treatment continued by making as much as will admit it. The man who can effect both objects is rarely to be found." He sought that rarity—an overseer both humane and productive—in Maryland, where, because of the mixture of free and slave labor, "the farmers there understand the management of negroes on a rational and humane plan."[55] But the tenures of his Maryland overseers were short and, for unknown reasons, not happy.

In 1799 Jefferson wrote: "I am not fit to be a farmer with the kind of labour that we have." And in the same period he indicted the labor system that harmonized so imperfectly with the systematic agricultural reforms he tried to introduce on his plantations: "My last revulsion from retirement has overshadowed me with despair when I contemplate the necessity of reformation in my farms. That work finds obstacles enough in the ignorance and unwillingness of the instruments employed, even in the presence of the master. But when he is obliged to be absent the half of every year no hope remains of that steady perserverence in a fixed plan which alone can ensure it's success."[56] After the overseer experiment of the 1790s, the "instruments employed"—the men and women who labored in Monticello's fields—had to take their chances with a long succession of local overseers.

In the summer of 1806 one of Jefferson's tradesmen stepped out of character. Joe Fossett startled him by running away from Monticello just five days after Jefferson returned from Washington. He sent his head carpenter "in pursuit of a young mulatto man, called Joe, 26. years of age, who ran away from here the night of the 29th. inst[ant] without the least word of difference with any body, and indeed having never in his life recieved a blow from any one." His disbelief at this insubordination from one of his most privileged slaves was soon modified by a glimmer of understanding. "We know he has taken the road towards Washington," Jefferson continued. "He may possibly trump up some story to be taken care of at the President's house till he can make up his mind which way to go, or perhaps he may make himself known to Edy only, as he was formerly connected with her."[57]

Fossett's uncharacteristic action forced Jefferson to consider, for a moment, that his slave had a life of his own. Fossett had not been running away from Monticello. He ran *to* the President's House, where Edy had been in training under a French chef since 1802. Fossett's desperate journey was evidently precipitated by something he heard from two hired slaves who had accompanied Jefferson from

The President's House in Washington, by Benjamin Henry Latrobe, 1817 (Library of Congress).

Washington. The situation may have been similar to that of the wagoner Davy and his wife Fanny, as remembered by Edmund Bacon. Fanny, too, was a trainee cook at the President's House and she and her husband "got into a terrible quarrel. Davy was jealous of his wife, and, I reckon, with good reason." Bacon was summoned to take them to Alexandria to be sold. "They wept, and begged, and made good promises, and made such an ado, that they begged the old gentleman out of it. But it was a good lesson for them."[58]

The pressures of separation had nearly destroyed the relationship of Davy and Fanny, who saw each other two or three times a year when he carted trees and plants or led horses to and from Washington. Joe and Edy, on the other hand, may have seen each other very little, if at all, between at least 1802 and Joe's sudden appearance in 1806. Any necessary repairs to their relationship were made quickly, for shortly after his arrival, Fossett was caught by Jefferson's Irish coachman leaving the President's House and put in jail. No record has survived of the reception the runaway met on his return to Monticello, where he waited three more years for Edy to return with the retiring President. There they renewed their connection and raised eight children.[59]

"In the Mountain with Old Master"[60]

The descendants of Joe Fossett and his relatives still tell stories about the starring roles played by their ancestors in the momentous events of the summer of 1781. The hero of one tale was the Monticello blacksmith who foiled the pursuing British dragoons by shoeing Jefferson's horse backwards. Other family members took part in the preservation of the family silver. In one version, the blacksmith's wife devised a scheme for hanging the valuables on iron hooks in the well. In another story a slave, in the act of secreting the silver, is trapped under the front portico by the arrival of Banastre Tarleton's troops. Joe Fossett, then actually only seven months old, is given the part of bringing this man food and water for two days, until the enemy leaves the mountain.[61]

These family traditions carried down through the generations the memory of skills and ingenuity that enabled slaves to participate in epic world events and made them indispensable to their master. They also reveal the slaves' consciousness of the larger stage on which their master moved. The dash southward along Carter's Mountain in 1781 may not have been Jefferson's finest hour, but the participants in the events of the first days of June knew the importance of preventing the governor's capture. Isaac Jefferson, taken to Philadephia in the early 1790s to learn tinsmithing, actually saw his master in action as a public man in his many-windowed house on Market Street, and, in memory, promoted him to President. As Martha Randolph remembered, the Monticello slaves believed her father to be "one of the greatest, and they knew him to be one of the best men and the kindest of masters."[62]

Jefferson would probably not have been able to reciprocate with tales of those living around him on the much smaller stage of Monticello. To protect himself from the realities of owning human beings, he needed the same psychological buffers as other well-intentioned slaveholders. The constant tension between self-interest and humanity seems to have induced in him a gradual closing of the imagination that distanced and dehumanized the black families of Monticello.

His records demonstrate this limited view. In the infrequent descriptive phrases of his correspondence, his slaves are singled out for characteristics—trustworthiness or unreliability, intelligence or stupidity, sobriety or drunkenness—that bear entirely on performance.[63] In the *Farm Book* they are given only first names, and diminutives at that. The husband and wife known as Joseph and Edith Fossett to their family members were just Joe and Edy to Jefferson. If Israel Jefferson's reminiscences had not been recorded by an eager journalist in 1873, we would never have known that the Ned and Jenny of Jefferson's records knew themselves as Edward and Jane Gillett. A negative picture emerges from correspondence with overseers and family members. There are discussions of misbehavior rather than comments on craftsmanship. Illness fills many pages, along with descriptions of the death throes of several slaves. Even Jupiter, Jefferson's lifelong companion as manservant and coachman, passed from the scene accompanied by words that demonstrated the inextricable connection between his humanity and his value as part of the labor force. Jefferson wrote that "I am sorry for him as well as sensible he leaves a void in my administration which I cannot fill up."[64]

Jefferson lived long enough to become fully entangled in the net of slavery's realities. His unsuccessful early efforts to curb or end slavery were followed by years in which he uttered simultaneous protestations of the impracticability of emancipation and cries of alarm about the consequences of inaction. The man who in 1786 wrote of "a bondage, one hour of which is fraught with more misery" than ages of the tyranny that American revolutionaries had just thrown off, was not the man who in 1814 told Thomas Cooper that American slaves "are better fed ..., warmer clothed, and labor less than the journeymen or day-laborers of England," living "without want, or the fear of it." His insights into the kinds of behavior caused by enslavement were forgotten and his suspicions of racial inferiority gained the upper hand, perhaps serving as a defense against stings of conscience. While Jefferson was shocked at the sight of French and German women driving the plows and hoeing the fields of Europe—it was "a barbarous perversion of the natural destination of the two sexes"—he never expressed misgivings about the long days of hard agricultural labor of the women he owned. His farms always were cultivated by "gangs of half men and half women." According to one visiting Englishman, Jefferson expressed the opinion in 1807 that the "Negro race were ... made to carry burthens." He appears to have convinced himself that those who were, as he suspected in print in the *Notes on Virginia*, "inferior in the faculties of reason and imagination," and whose griefs were "transient," might find happiness in a bondage mitigated by a benevolent hand.[65]

Jefferson's own efforts turned to reforming slavery rather than ending it. In 1787 he wanted to put his slaves "ultimately on an easier footing," and five years later his experiment with Maryland overseers was inaugurated in order to place his slaves "on the comfortable footing of the laborers of other countries." While in Paris he briefly contemplated importing Germans to settle on fifty-acre farms, "intermingled" with his slaves, and "all on the footing of the Metayers [tenants who pay in kind] of Europe" (he prefaced this proposal with his opinion that freeing slaves was "like abandoning children"). But the overriding demands of debt made even his reform efforts contingent on the impossible. The ultimate "easier footing" could be realized only after the slaves "have paid the debts" due from the Wayles estate. In 1792, when the Maryland overseer plan was aired, the improved treatment of the slaves was made to depend on their own exertions; they must "make as much as will admit" the continuation of better conditions.[66]

Neither Jefferson nor his slaves ever succeeded in clearing away his massive debts, which only grew with the years. It is impossible to know, partly because his exact intentions were not expressed, just how much he was able to carry out his wish to ameliorate the condition of his own slaves, to contribute to their happiness as he perceived it. There is plentiful evidence, however, that the Monticello slaves were made more "comfortable" in bondage than most of their fellows, even in Virginia.

Edith Fossett returned to these conditions in the spring of 1809. She probably moved into the cook's room—a ten by fourteen foot space with brick floor in the stone-built south dependencies of the main house. Two other rooms there were occupied by slaves, but most lived in log cabins on Mulberry Row or elsewhere on the mountain slopes. A visitor from Washington in 1809, although struck by "a most unpleasant contrast" between the slave dwellings and the neoclassical "palace" standing together on the levelled summit of Monticello, declared that "they are much better than I have seen on any other plantation." Their superiority could not have been due to their size or materials—they varied from twelve to fourteen feet wide and fourteen to twenty feet long, had wooden chimneys and earth floors. Perhaps they were more carefully built and maintained. In 1809 Peter Hemings was to remove to a cabin on Mulberry Row, fitted up "in an entirely comfortable and decent manner," and instructions to overseers regularly mention the winter "mending" of slave cabins.[67]

Kitchen at Monticello (Robert C. Lautman).

Despite the hours she spent each day in the main kitchen, Edy Fossett still received the normal weekly food rations—a peck of cornmeal and a pound of pork, but she was probably able to vary this monotonous fare for her family with kitchen leftovers and her own skills. Her clothing allowance was similar to that on other southern plantations—two outfits a year, cotton for summer and a mixture of cotton and wool for winter; a striped blanket was issued once every three years. From at least 1815, when raw cotton prices were high, the summer cloth for her children was woven from a mixture of cotton and hemp.[68]

During the years of Jefferson's final retirement to Monticello, Edy and Joe Fossett filled two of the most important positions on the mountain. Almost a century later, Peter Fossett remembered that his mother was "Mr. Jefferson's favorite cook" and his father "had charge of all mechanical work done on the estate." Edy took over the new kitchen and prepared meals for a mounting flood of guests. While visitors' accounts are disappointingly vague about the food, all agreed on the quality of the fare. "The dinner was always choice, and served in the French style," wrote Bostonian George Ticknor. Daniel Webster recorded in 1824 that "dinner is served in half Virginian, half French style, in good taste and abundance."[69]

Joe Fossett ran the Mulberry Row blacksmith shop, which served the neighborhood as well as the master of Monticello. He was allowed to keep a shilling in every dollar of shop income, and earned additional money by making chain traces

Mulberry Row, once lined with at least seventeen structures, including workshops and dwellings for enslaved and free workmen (H. Andrew Johnson).

	Length of Day in Hours	Linen task	Wool task	Cotton task
Jan. Dec.	9.	15. oz.	12. oz.	6. oz.
Feb. Nov.	10.	16 ⅔	13 ⅓	6 ⅔
Mar. Oct.	11.	18 ⅓	14 ⅔	7 ⅓
Apr. Sep.	12.	20.	16.	8.
May. Aug.	13.	21 ⅔	17 ⅓	8 ⅔
June July.	14.	23 ⅓	18 ⅔	9 ½
Average	11½	19.	15⅓	7 ⅔

Jefferson's chart of the daily tasks of the spinners in his textile shop (Farm Book; courtesy of the Massachusetts Historical Society).

and plating saddle trees for a Charlottesville blacksmith in his free time. Fossett's work day, like that of most other Monticello slaves, lasted from dawn to dusk. Jefferson's chart of the daily tasks of his textile workers indicates that their labors grew from nine hours in the darkest winter months to fourteen hours in the longest days of June and July. Jobs that were tasked could provide early release for fast workers but, when the tasks were set by Jefferson the maximizer, could also lead to even longer work days. "Jerry says that you tell him that he is to bring a certain number of logs a day," wrote Edmund Bacon, "and that it takes him till after night to do it." Bacon drew this situation to Jefferson's attention for the sake of the mules, not the wagoner.[70]

It is apparent that for many of the Monticello slaves a second working day began after dark. Mothers had to attend to their households, preparing meals, repairing clothing, and caring for their children. Both men and women pursued activities to supplement the standard of living provided by their master. Every slave household at Monticello had a poultry yard and most raised their own vegetables. A typical Sunday is revealed in the household account book kept by one of Jefferson's granddaughters. Slaves carried to the mountaintop their chickens and eggs, cabbages and watermelons, to stock the Monticello kitchen, and took home dimes and half-bits in exchange. Some probably obtained passes so they could take their products into Charlottesville for sale as well.[71]

The nearby river and surrounding forests also provided opportunities for additional food or money. Hunting and trapping expeditions yielded raccoons, possums, and squirrels to add to the pot and skins to be sold. Isaac Jefferson's brother Bagwell, a farm laborer, makes several appearances in Jefferson's accounts, selling him skins for a bellows, fish, ducks, hops, timothy seed, watermelons, cucumbers, and cymlin squash. Jefferson's grandson regaled his children with tales of midnight forays as a boy after possum and honey, in the company of the black men. After the

Jefferson's granddaughter Anne Cary Randolph records household purchases from Monticello slaves, August 1806 (Library of Congress).

dogs treed their quarry or a bee tree was felled they returned to sit around the fire in a slave cabin. At "a little table covered with the best," one of the wives provided "a pot of hot coffee, fried meat and eggs, and a dish of honey."[72]

The pleasures of the quarters received little comment in the correspondence of Jefferson and his family. Apparently without curfews, his slaves took advantage of the freedom of the night. Jefferson observed, in the *Notes on Virginia*, that "a black, after hard labour through the day, will be induced by the slightest amusements to sit up till midnight, or later, though knowing he must be out with the first dawn of the morning." He knew his gardener John as a "great nightwalker" and thus unsuitable as a guardian for the main house. Former slave Isaac Jefferson remembered that his master's brother Randolph would "come out among black people, play the fiddle and dance half the night."[73]

There are further suggestions of the solace of music. Three of Sally Hemings's sons were noted musicians. Her oldest, Beverly (b. 1798), played fiddle in the South Pavilion for the Saturday night dances of Jefferson's granddaughters and young men at school nearby. He may also have provided the single note of holiday spirit in the quiet Christmas of 1821. Mary Randolph wrote her sister: "I have not had a single application to write passes ... and except catching the sound of a fiddle yesterday on my way to the smokehouse and getting a glimpse of the fiddler as he stood with half closed eyes and head thrown back with one foot keeping time to his own scraping in the midst of a circle of attentive and admiring auditors I have not seen or heard any thing like Christmas gambols."[74]

The most remarkable evidence of the vigorous music and storytelling tradition in the Monticello quarters survives because of an interested foreigner and one member of Jefferson's household. His daughter Martha, who at fourteen had written her father, "I wish with all my soul that the poor negroes were all freed," was primed by the tales and songs of her childhood nurse. Even late in life, she had not lost her sensitivity to both the conditions and culture of the slave community around her. She shared cornshelling and rowing songs and tales of Mr. Fox and Mr. Rabbit with interested visitors to Monticello. In the year she died Martha Randolph worried about the fate of some of her slaves, hoping to protect them from the laxer morals of the vicinity of the University of Virginia: "I feel anxious that these poor uneducated creatures should be placed in situations as little exposed to temptation as possible."[75]

The younger members of Jefferson's household made some of the only recorded efforts to enlighten those "poor uneducated creatures." Madison Hemings recalled learning his ABCs from Jefferson's granddaughters, while Joe Fossett's son Peter learned his letters from Jefferson's grandson Meriwether Lewis Randolph. Ellen Randolph wrote in 1819 that she was "anxious to have it in my power to befriend, and educate as well as I can" one of the motherless daughters of Monticello butler Burwell Colbert. In the absence of explicit statements on the subject, Jefferson's own attitude toward the education of his slaves is harder to determine. His missing response to Quaker activist Robert Pleasants's 1796 plan for instructing black children seems to have recommended delay. The only emancipation plan Jefferson considered feasible called for education, at public expense, in "tillage, arts or sciences, according to their geniusses," followed by deportation. This plan required the permanent separation of children from their parents, a necessity that

Jefferson agreed would produce "some scruples of humanity, but this would be straining at a gnat, and swallowing a camel."[76]

Closer to home, Jefferson's never-executed tenancy plan called merely for bringing up the children "in habits of property and foresight." The blacks' apparent absence of foresight weighed heavily in Jefferson's mind as a stumbling block to emancipation. It colored his discussion of racial characteristics in the *Notes on Virginia* and he brought it forth in conversation with visiting foreigners. A bemused British diplomat listened in 1807 to Jefferson's favorite example of the lack of forethought demonstrated by his own slaves. At the approach of summer they cast off their blankets, "without a thought as to what may become of them, wherever they may happen to be at the time, and then not seldom lose them in the woods or the fields from mere carelessness." No slave in the upper south took blankets lightly, so it is possible that Monticello's blanket-tossers may have counted on Jefferson's willingness to replace their loss. It is even more likely that some of these apparently thoughtless slaves had discovered a way to acquire extra blankets for warmth or sale. Jefferson himself had noted, in 1806, that a recent Monticello overseer had failed to distribute a single blanket during his five-year tenure. This experience may have caused the very opposite of what the master saw—an effort to prepare for an unpredictable future.[77]

Israel Gillett, a twenty-four-year-old postilion, overheard Jefferson tell the Marquis de Lafayette that slaves should be taught to read but not to write, as that would "enable them to forge papers, when they could no longer be kept in subjugation." The statement Israel recalled, almost fifty years after the event, is difficult to verify. A number of Jefferson's slaves could read *and* write. John Hemings's surviving letters report on his joinery work at Poplar Forest, his brother James left an inventory of the Monticello kitchen, and there is one letter from Hannah, a Poplar Forest household slave. Several others could at least read: Jefferson left written instructions in his absences for the carpenters John and Davy and Great George the overseer. Albemarle County records reveal that Mary Hemings Bell and Joseph Fossett could sign their names and probably could read and write, although they may have learned after they were freed.[78] It is not known how these slaves learned their letters, nor is there any direct evidence that Jefferson took an active role in educating the African-

John Hemings to Thomas Jefferson, 28 Sep. 1825 (courtesy of the Massachusetts Historical Society).

American children around him.[79] There is also no sign that he took up his own challenge in the *Notes on Virginia* or emulated the example of his mentor George Wythe, by testing the intellectual powers of blacks through the cultivation of their minds in improved conditions. One clue to this vacuum appears in a letter Jefferson wrote questioning the educational aims of the African Institution of London: "I wish they may begin their work at the right end. Our experience with the Indians has proved that letters are not the first, but the last step in the progression from barbarism to civilisation."[80]

Religious instruction of slaves would, of course, have been completely unJeffersonian. The life of the spirit was pursued beyond the control of the master and thus escaped his commentary. Again it is the negative events that inspired the scattered references that can only suggest the vitality of religious beliefs in the Monticello slave community. Jefferson's granddaughter Mary complained of having to watch a visitor's children one Sunday because "mammy is gone *'to meeting.'*" Her sister told of the death of Priscilla Hemings, longtime head nurse in the Jefferson-Randolph household, whose last hours included "a prayer meeting at her house" and a Bible reading before bedtime by her husband John. African traditional beliefs are

also evident, mainly in discussions of the ill effects of the prescriptions of black doc-
tors—almost universally labeled "poisons" in Jefferson's papers.[81]

There were two worlds at Monticello, where medicine and beliefs in one were
perceived as poison and superstition in the other. Jefferson had no access to the hidden world of his slaves, but they were a constant presence in his, listening and
watching. From the slave women in the
house to Israel on the carriage horse, they
attended to all words and actions that
might play a part in shaping their future.
Joe Fossett, in the blacksmith shop—the
closest thing to a neighborhood gathering
place—may have been a monitor for the
mountain, listening for assessments of the
state of Jefferson's finances, so critical to the
stability of the Monticello slave community. One of Lafayette's companions talked
to the slaves in 1824, when they told him
they were "perfectly happy, that they were
subject to no ill-treatment, that their tasks
were very easy, and that they cultivated the

*Tombstone of Priscilla Hemings (d. 1830),
Monticello head nurse and wife of John Hemings
(Thomas Jefferson Memorial Foundation).*

lands of Monticello with the greater pleasure, because they were almost sure of not
being torn away from them, to be transported elsewhere, so long as Mr. Jefferson
lived."[82]

INDEPENDENCE

On July 4, 1827, one year after Jefferson's death, Joseph Fossett became a free
man. Six months earlier Jefferson's granddaughter Mary had reported to a sister the
results of the Monticello dispersal sale: "The negroes with one exception I believe,
are all sold to persons living in the state, many of them in this neighbourhood or the
adjoining counties, and most of them I believe also, are well and satisfactorily
placed, as much to their own wishes as they could be in leaving our estate." No reference was made to the breaking up of families this satisfactory placement entailed.

Joe Fossett had watched his wife and children sold to at least four different bidders. Edy and their two youngest children William and Daniel were bought by Jesse Scott; twelve-year-old Peter's new master was John R. Jones; fifteen-year-old Elizabeth Ann was sold to Charlottesville merchant John Winn; and University of Virginia professor Charles Bonnycastle bought seventeen-year-old Patsy. The fates of three other siblings are unknown.[83]

Jefferson had described Fossett at the time of his 1806 escapade as "strong and resolute," characteristics greatly needed in his first years of freedom. The fragmentary records suggest that he worked at his trade with a steadiness demanded by his need to reunite his scattered family and prepare for removal beyond the boundaries of slavery. Spared the requirement to leave the state within a year by an act of assembly requested in Jefferson's will, he continued to pursue his blacksmithing trade in Albemarle County. He may even have remained in the Mulberry Row blacksmith shop until 1831, when Monticello was sold to James T. Barclay and Fossett bought a lot in Charlottesville with a shop on it.[84]

At some time before September 15, 1837, Joe Fossett became the owner of his wife, five of their children (two born subsequent to the sale), and four grandchildren, for on that date he manumitted them all. It is apparent that the key to family unity was Joe Fossett's mother, Mary Hemings Bell. She and her children by merchant Thomas Bell had shared in Bell's estate in 1800 and her daughter Sally had married Jesse Scott in 1802. Thus, it was probably the combined resources of Scott and the Bells that provided the $505 for the purchase of Edy and the two youngest children—and probably also the money for the purchase of the third child, Elizabeth Ann.[85]

It is evident that, beginning in the 1780s, when Mary Hemings was leased and then sold to Thomas Bell, the Monticello slave community had a toehold in the more complex free community of Charlottesville. Thomas Bell's

Receipts from sale of Fossett family at January 1827 auction (courtesy of Mrs. James C. Moyer).

house on Main Street, occupied by his "widow," then her daughter and son-in-law Sally Jefferson Bell and Jesse Scott, and their children, was the residence of Hemingses for a century.[86] Jesse Scott, a free man of color said to be part-Indian, and his sons, the "famous fiddling Scotts," enliv-ened dances at the University of Virginia, at the Hot and White Sulphur Springs, and throughout the state for a good part of the century. In 1888 Ora Langhorne paid a visit to the last surviving member of "the Scott minstrels, long famous throughout the South and well known to all visitors at the Virginia springs." Robert Scott reported that "the taste for music shown by his family had early attracted Mr. Jefferson's notice, as he dearly loved music himself, and he had taken much kindly interest in the family .... Mr. Jefferson had always been very kind to [Jesse Scott] and had encouraged him to have his children educated."[87]

Jesse Scott (1781–1862), a celebrated fiddler, purchased his brother-in-law Joseph Fossett's wife and children in 1827. Artist unknown (courtesy of Olivia S. Dutcher).

Peter Fossett was not one of the children his father was able to purchase and free before the family left for Ohio about 1840. He remained a slave for over twenty years after Jefferson's death, making at least two at-tempts to run away. The learning he had gleaned from his years as "a sort of family pet" in the Monticello household was increased by enlisting the aid of his new master's sons. Then Peter Fossett passed his knowledge on to a fellow slave by the light of pine knots, stealing away to a deserted cabin long after everyone else was asleep. Finally, again by the combined efforts of members of an extended network of kin, he was able to purchase his freedom and join his family in Cincinnati.[88]

Peter Fossett's story demonstrates the extent to which identity is buried by the dehumanizing institution of slavery. In freedom his life is known, and becomes an expression of much that cannot be known about the rest of the Monticello slave community. Flourishing unrecorded in the Monticello quarters were singular skills, a hunger for education, powerful bonds of family and community, and deep reli-gious beliefs. Peter Fossett became "the most prominent of the early caterers" in

Cincinnati, worked with Levi Coffin in the Underground Railroad, and has been called a "father" of the Ohio black Baptist church. His flock at First Baptist Church helped him satisfy a desire, at age eighty-five, to return to his birthplace. In 1900, the "last surviving slave of Thomas Jefferson," who had abandoned him in 1826, was welcomed to the entrance hall of Monticello.[89]

Rev. Peter Fossett (1815–1900), son of Joseph and Edith Fossett, Monticello's head blacksmith and cook (Wendell P. Dabney, Cincinnati's Colored Citizens, Cincinnati, 1926).

ACKNOWLEGEMENTS AND NOTES

This essay first appeared as "'Those Who Labor for My Happiness': Thomas Jefferson and His Slaves," in *Jeffersonian Legacies*, ed. Peter S. Onuf (Charlottesville: University Press of Virginia, 1993), pp. 147-80.

I would like to thank the Virginia Foundation for the Humanities and the Thomas Jefferson Memorial Foundation for their support of work on a related project. I could not have written this essay without those months spent considering the lives of Jefferson's slaves. I am also grateful to Peter Onuf, for suggestions about structure that were vital to the final product.

In my work on this subject I am following trails already blazed by others, notably James A. Bear, Jr., whose longtime interest in the Hemings family of Monticello has nourished my curiosity and informed far more of his work than the directly relevant "The Hemings Family of Monticello," *Virginia Cavalcade* 29, no. 2 (autumn 1979):78-87. Other useful accounts of the African-American residents of Monticello include "To Possess Living Souls," chapter four in Jack McLaughlin, *Jefferson and Monticello: The Biography of a Builder* (New York, 1988), pp. 94-145, and Elizabeth Langhorne, "The Other Hemings," *Albemarle Magazine* (Oct./Nov. 1980), 59-66, and "A Black Family at Monticello," *Magazine of Albemarle County History* 43 (1985):1-16. Note that in her discussion of the fate of Sally Hemings after Jefferson's death, in the latter article and in chapter 37 of *Monticello: A Family Story* (Chapel Hill, 1987), Langhorne mistakes her for another Sally at Monticello. Material on Jefferson and Monticello contributes to an excellent discussion of larger issues in Mary Beth Norton, Herbert G. Gutman, and Ira Berlin, "The Afro-American Family in the Age of Revolution," *Slavery and Freedom in the Age of the American Revolution*, ed. Ira Berlin and Ronald Hoffman (Urbana, 1986), pp. 175-191. Beware, however, of Table 3 on page 184, which credits Jefferson with twice as many slaves as he actually had. More recently there is much fascinating new information mixed with an unfortunate number of errors in Judith P. Justus, *Down From the Mountain: The Oral History of the Hemings Family* (Perrysburg, OH, 1990).

The following short titles are used for frequently cited works in this essay:

FB   Thomas Jefferson's "Farm Book," reproduced in facsimile in *FBB*.

FBB   Edwin M. Betts, ed., *Thomas Jefferson's Farm Book*, Princeton, 1953.

GB   Edwin M. Betts, ed., *Thomas Jefferson's Garden Book*, Philadelphia, 1944.

MB   James A. Bear, Jr., and Lucia C. Stanton, eds., *Jefferson's Memorandum Books: Accounts, with Legal Records and Miscellany*, 1767-1826, Princeton, forthcoming

Boyd   Julian P. Boyd et al., eds., *The Papers of Thomas Jefferson*, 26 vols. to date, Princeton, 1950-.

Ford   Paul Leicester Ford, ed., *The Works of Thomas Jefferson*, 12 vols. [Federal Edition], New York, 1904-5.

L&B   Andrew A. Lipscomb and Albert Ellery Bergh, eds., *The Writings of Thomas Jefferson*, 20 vols., Washington, 1903-4.

LofA   Thomas Jefferson, *Writings*, ed. Merrill D. Peterson [Library of America], New York, 1984.

[1] TJ to Edward Bancroft, 26 Jan. 1789, *Boyd*, 14:492.

[2] Charlottesville *Central Gazette*, 13 Jan. 1827. Only fragmentary documentation survives for the January 1827 sale. Transactions are mentioned in occasional letters and in almost thirty sales slips, which note the purchase of only thirty-four slaves (Monticello Dispersal Sale receipts, University of Virginia Library [hereafter ViU], 5291). Apparently all 130 slaves were not actually sold in 1827, as an account of a second sale of 33 slaves, 1 Jan. 1829, also survives (ViU: 8937).

[3] Mary J. Randolph to Ellen Coolidge, 25 Jan. 1827, ViU; Thomas Jefferson Randolph reminiscences, ViU: 1397. Randolph actually attended the sale; his sister Mary did not.

[4] *FB*, p. 27.

[5] TJ to Henry Rose, 23 Oct. 1801, *FBB*, p. 18; TJ to Craven Peyton, 14 Nov. 1819, *FBB*, p. 145; TJ to James Madison, 26 July 1806, Library of Congress (hereafter DLC); TJ to M. B. Jefferson, 2 Aug. 1815, *FBB*, p. 39.

[6] Because of his surname, it has been suggested that Joseph Fossett may have been the son of William Fossett, a white carpenter working at Monticello from 1775 to 1779 (MB 11 Feb. 1775, 5 Aug. and 12 Sep. 1779). Some of Joseph Fossett's descendants make the claim that Jefferson was his father (see Lerone Bennett, "Thomas Jefferson's Negro Grandchildren," *Ebony* 10 (Nov. 1954): 78-80). Betty Hemings may actually have had eleven children at this time. Lee Marmon, researcher for Poplar Forest, makes the plausible suggestion that Doll (b. 1757), wife of Abraham, a carpenter, was her daughter ("Poplar Forest Research Report," part 3, Aug. 1991, p. 39).

[7] Jefferson inaugurated his *Farm Book* with three lists of slaves at the time of the division of the Wayles estate: the first, a roll of his own 52 slaves in Albemarle County; the second, the 135 Wayles slaves and their locations; the third, a list of the combined total of 187, with new locations in three counties (*FB*, pp. 5-18). In 1782 his Albemarle County total was 129, behind Edward Carter with 242 slaves and ahead of the estate of Robert Carter Nicholas, with 120 slaves (Lester J. Cappon, "Personal Property Tax List of Albemarle County, 1782," *Magazine of Albemarle County History* 5 [1944-45]:54,69,72). After the sale of his Goochland and Cumberland county lands in the 1790s, Jefferson's slave property was usually distributed in a ratio of three to two between his Albemarle and Bedford county estates—both about 5,000 acres. The combined totals for 1796, 1810, and 1815 were 167, 199, and 223 ("Jefferson's Slaves: Approximate Total Numbers," 8 Mch. 1990, Monticello Research Department). Auctions accounted for the sale of 71 slaves from his Goochland and Bedford county plantations, 14 more were sold to individuals, and 76 were given to his sister and daughters on their marriages ("Negroes alienated from 1784. to 1794," Feinstone Collection, David Library of the American Revolution, on deposit at American Philosophical Society; this document is no doubt the missing page 25 of Jefferson's *Farm Book*).

8 TJ to John Wayles Eppes, 30 June 1820, ViU. On this particular occasion, he was grateful for Eppes's offer to buy slaves without moving them from Poplar Forest. This kept them "in the family." Isaac Jefferson's mother Ursula was bought at the request of Martha Jefferson, because she was "a favorite house woman"; Jefferson purchased Nance Hemings the weaver on the resumption of textile production in 1795; and young men were needed for the digging of his canal in the 1790s (TJ to Archibald Thweatt, 29 May 1810, DLC; TJ to W. Callis, 8 May 1795, ViU; MB 26 Mch. 1797, 6 May 1805; TJ to John Jordan, 21 Dec. 1805, *FBB*, p. 21).

9 Jordan to TJ, 4 Dec. 1805, Massachusetts Historical Society, hereafter MHi; TJ to Jordan, 21 Dec. 1805 and 9 Feb. 1806, *FBB*, pp. 21-22.

10 TJ to Randolph Lewis, 23 Apr. 1807, *FBB*, p. 26; TJ to Jeremiah Goodman, 6 Jan. 1815, *GB*, p. 540. This letter also suggests that Jefferson instructed his overseers to make some efforts to control behavior. Goodman, who interpreted the "home" rule too strictly, repeatedly "drove" Phill Hubbard from his wife Hanah's house and punished her for receiving him. Hubbard and his wife lived on different plantations, but both were part of the Poplar Forest estate. Jefferson intervened to facilitate their union.

11 TJ to Thomas Cooper, 10 Sep. 1814, *L&B*, 14:183; Frederick Douglass, *Life and Times* (1881, repr. New York, 1983), p. 89.

12 TJ to Edward Coles, 25 Aug. 1814, *FBB*, p. 39; Thomas Mann Randolph to TJ, 6 Mch. 1802, MHi; Martha J. Randolph to Nicholas P. Trist, 7 Mch. 1822, University of North Carolina Library.

13 TJ to Joel Yancey, 17 Jan. 1819, MHi. Another statement expressing the value of slave women as producers of "capital" appears in TJ to John Wayles Eppes, 30 June 1820, ViU.

14 *FB*, pp. 5, 52; TJ to Jeremiah Goodman, 5 Mch. 1813, *FBB*, p. 483; "Negroes alienated from 1784. to 1794.", Feinstone Collection, American Philosophical Society.

15 TJ to Randolph Jefferson, 25 Sep. 1792, *Boyd*, 24:416; TJ to Thomas Mann Randolph, 12 Oct. 1792, *Boyd*, 24:473; "Negroes alienated from 1784. to 1794."; TJ to W. Callis, 8 May 1795, ViU; *FB*, p. 24. Critta (c1783-1819) eventually came to Monticello as the wife of the butler Burwell Colbert.

16 TJ to Nicholas Lewis, 12 Apr. 1792, *Boyd*, 23:408; "Negroes alienated from 1784. to 1794." Bell, whom Jefferson called "a man remarkeable for his integrity," acknowledged paternity of Bob and Sally and left his property in a life estate to Mary Hemings Wells [Wayles?] Bell in his will (TJ to William Short, 13 Apr. 1800, Swem Library, College of William and Mary; Albemarle County Will Book, 4:59-60).

17 Martha Randolph to TJ, 16 Jan. 1791, Edwin Morris Betts and James A. Bear, eds., *The Family Letters of Thomas Jefferson* (Columbia, Mo., 1966), p. 68.

18 *FB*, pp. 41, 49.

19 Thomas Jefferson Randolph to [Pike County *Republican*?], 1874, ViU: 8937; James A. Bear, Jr., ed., *Jefferson at Monticello* (Charlottesville, 1967), pp. 99-100; author's translation of F. A. F. La Rochefoucauld-Liancourt, *Voyage dans les Etats-Unis d'Amerique* (Paris, 1798/99), 5:35. I use this in preference to the 1799 London edition, which, for in-

stance, translates "*quarterons*" as "mongrel negroes." The Comte de Volney also observed at Monticello, in the same summer, slave children "as white as I am" (Jean Gaulmier, *L'Ideologue Volney*, 1951, repr. Paris, 1980, p. 371).

[20] Madison Hemings's recollections (Fawn M. Brodie, *Thomas Jefferson: An Intimate Biography*, New York, 1974, p. 471-72); Bear, *Jefferson at Monticello*, p. 4. Robert, James, Thenia, Critta, Peter, and Sally were allegedly the children of Jefferson's father-in-law John Wayles. In the words of Isaac Jefferson, "Folks said that these Hemingses was old Mr. Wayles's children" (Bear, *Jefferson at Monticello*, p. 4). Madison Hemings stated the connection more emphatically in 1873. No reference to the Wayles-Hemings relationship has been found in the papers of Jefferson or his family. John Hemings was said to have been the son of Joseph Neilson, a white joiner resident at Monticello from 1775 to 1779 (Brodie, *Jefferson*, p. 475; MB 28 Jan. 1775, 12 Sep. 1779).

[21] The story that Jefferson was the father of slaves by Sally Hemings was first published by James Thomson Callender in the Richmond *Recorder* in the fall of 1802. It was carried through the nineteenth century in Federalist attacks, British critiques of American democracy, and abolitionist efforts to end slavery. Fawn Brodie's biography of 1974 revived the claim and suggested a romantic dimension—that the connection was not exploitative but a meaningful thirty-eight-year union. Oral traditions originating with the children of Sally Hemings strongly support the connection; Jefferson's daughter and grandchildren believed it a moral impossibility and suggested Jefferson's Carr nephews as more likely suspects. Both sides received their contemporary supporters and Jefferson himself seems to have privately denied the charge in an 1805 letter to Robert Smith. Sources on the controversy include Douglass Adair, "The Jefferson Scandals," in *Fame and the Founding Fathers*, ed. Trevor Colbourn (New York, 1974), pp. 160-91; Fawn Brodie's biography and her articles in *American Heritage* (23, no. 4 [June 1971]: 48-57, 97-100; 27, no. 6 [Oct. 1976]: 29-33, 94-99); Virginius Dabney, *The Jefferson Scandals: A Rebuttal* (New York, 1981); Dumas Malone, "Mr. Jefferson's Private Life," reprinted from *Proceedings of the American Antiquarian Society*, Apr. 1974; Minnie Shumate Woodson, *The Sable Curtain* (Washington, 1985), appendix. Michael Durey has recently somewhat refurbished Callender's image, demonstrating the likelihood that Callender took the story from what he considered reliable sources rather than making it up (Michael Durey, "*With the Hammer of Truth*": *James Thomson Callender and America's Early National Heroes* [Charlottesville, 1990], pp. 157-63). Also, another birth date has come to light. Sally Hemings's daughter Thenia, who did not survive infancy, was born about 7 Dec. 1799; Jefferson returned to Monticello from Philadelphia on 8 Mch. 1799 (TJ to John Wayles Eppes, 21 Dec. 1799, ViU; *FB*, p. 56)

[22] Samuel Shepherd, *The Statutes at Large of Virginia* (Richmond, 1835) 1: 123; TJ to Francis Calley Gray, 4 Mch. 1815, DLC.

[23] Bear, *Jefferson at Monticello*, pp. 102, 122; *FB*, p. 130; Ellen Wayles Coolidge to Joseph Coolidge, 24 Oct. 1858, Coolidge letterbook, pp. 98-99, ViU. She cited the cases of "three young men and one girl" (Harriet Hemings). Besides Beverly Hemingses, one of the three men was probably James Hemings (b. 1787), son of Sally's sister Critta. When he ran away from Monticello in 1804, only persuasion was exerted in an unsuccessful effort to bring him back. He briefly reappeared at Monticello in 1815, apparently as a free man (MB 13 Oct. 1815).

[24] Gilbert Osofsky, ed., *Puttin' on Ole Massa* (New York, 1969), p. 64. Ellen Coolidge in 1858 blamed the "Irish workmen" building the Monticello house, "dissipated young men in the neighbourhood," and—in the case of the Hemingses—her own Carr uncles (Coolidge letterbook, pp. 100-102, ViU). Edmund Bacon reported that Thomas Jefferson Randolph's schoolmates were "intimate with the Negro women" (Bear, *Jefferson at Monticello*, p. 88). Although no indictments of individual overseers have been found, the overseer class often took the blame, as the Duc de La Rochefoucauld-Liancourt reported after his visit to Monticello in 1796 (*Voyage*, 5:35).

[25] TJ to William Short, 18 Jan. 1826, *Ford*, 12:434. See also TJ to James Monroe, 24 Nov. 1801, *Ford*, 9:317; TJ to Edward Coles, 25 Aug. 1814, *FBB*, p. 38. The Duc de La Rochefoucauld-Liancourt observed, in an unpublished paragraph of his travels, that fear of mixture lay at the root of Jefferson's reluctance to act on the emancipation issue: "The generous and enlightened Mr. Jefferson cannot but demonstrate a desire to see these negroes emancipated. But he sees so many difficulties in their emancipation even postponed, he adds so many conditions to render it practicable, that it is thus reduced to the impossible. He keeps for example the opinion he advanced in his notes, that the negroes of Virginia can only be emancipated all at once, and by exporting to a distance the whole of the black race. He bases this opinion on the certain danger, if there were nothing else, of seeing blood mixed without means of preventing it" (author's translation, Library of Congress microfilm of original manuscript in Bibliotheque Nationale).

[26] Jefferson's first slave, Sawney, bequeathed him by his father, was described as "mulatto" (Peter Jefferson will, 13 July 1757, Albemarle County Will Book, 2:33). So was Sandy, a carpenter who ran away from Shadwell in 1769 (advertisement, 7 Sep. 1769, *Boyd*, 1:33).

[27] Harvest rolls 1795-1800, *FB*, pp. 46, 58. At the time of Jefferson's death, Critta Hemings was married to free black Zachariah Bowles (Albemarle County Deed Book, XXII, 412) and Mary was living in the property left her by merchant Thomas Bell. John Hemings's wife Priscilla was head nurse in the household of Martha and Thomas Mann Randolph. Peter Hemings's wife was also probably a Randolph slave, as she and her children lived at Monticello in 1810, after the Randolphs had moved there from Edgehill (*FBB*, p. 134).

[28] "A slave...is born to live and labour for another," *Notes on the State of Virginia*, ed. William Peden (Chapel Hill, 1954), p. 163.

[29] TJ to J. B. Demeunier, 29 Apr. 1795, *Ford*, 8:174.

[30] *FB*, p. 111. Surviving nailery accounts are fragmentary. There are five pages of accounts, 1794 to 1796, bound with Jefferson's Ledger, 1767-1770, ViU, and a nailery account book, 1796-1800, in the William Andrews Clark Memorial Library, University of California at Los Angeles.

[31] Nailery account book, Clark Memorial Library.

[32] TJ to James Lyle, 10 July 1795, *FBB*, p. 430; TJ to J. B. Deumeunier, 29 Apr. 1795, *Ford*, 8:175.

[33] TJ to James Maury, 16 June 1815, *FBB*, p. 490; TJ to Nicholas Lewis, 11 July 1788, *Boyd*, 13:343; TJ to Mary Jefferson Eppes, 11 Apr. 1801, Betts and Bear, *Family Letters*, p. 201; TJ to Thomas Mann Randolph, 29 Jan. 1801, DLC.

[34] TJ to Thomas Mann Randolph, 3 Feb. 1793, MHi; memorandum to Jeremiah Goodman, Dec. 1811, *GB*, p. 467.

[35] TJ to Edmund Bacon, 6 Oct. 1806, MHi; Thomas Mann Randolph to TJ, 3 Jan. 1801, ViU; TJ to Randolph, 9 Jan. 1801, DLC; memorandum to Jeremiah Goodman, Dec. 1811, *GB*, p. 466.

[36] Bear, *Jefferson at Monticello*, p. 100; Ellen W. Randolph to Martha J. Randolph, 27 Sep. [1816?], ViU.

[37] *FB*, p. 77; TJ to George Jefferson, 3 Dec. 1801, *FBB*, p. 425; Bear, *Jefferson at Monticello*, p. 102; memorandum to Edmund Bacon, Oct. 1806, in Bear, p. 54.

[38] TJ to Thomas Mann Randolph, 19 May 1793, DLC; TJ to Thomas Munroe, 4 Mch. 1815, Henry E. Huntington Library. Dinsmore's inventory of the Monticello joinery in 1809, listing over eighty molding planes among its tools, is further testament to the extraordinary work done on the mountaintop (inventory, 15 Apr. 1809, MHi).

[39] TJ to Benjamin Austin, 9 Jan. 1816, *LofA*, p. 1371.

[40] "Reminiscences of Madison Hemings," Brodie, *Jefferson*, p. 474; Bear, *Jefferson at Monticello*, p. 23. In 1799 thirteen-year-old nailer Phil Hubbard got a weekly ration of half a pound of beef and four salt herring, while Ned, a farm laborer the same age, had to share three-quarters of a pound a beef and six herring with five younger brothers and sisters (*FB*, p. 57; see also p. 135, for special meat rations for children working in both the nailery and the textile shop in 1810).

[41] Nailery account book, Clark Memorial Library; MB 17 Mch. 1813. Davy, for instance, burnt a kiln of 40 cords that yielded 1,276 bushels of charcoal, or 32 bushels to the cord; Jefferson therefore paid him a "premium" of 32 times $.05, or $1.60 (MB 23 Apr. 1823).

[42] MB passim; see, for example, 11 Apr. 1811, 26 Oct. 1816, and 14 Apr. 1826.

[43] Thomas Mann Randolph to TJ, 22 Apr. 1798, ViU; TJ to Randolph, 15 Feb. 1798, 29 Jan. 1801, DLC; Randolph to TJ, 7 Feb. 1801, ViU; 3 Feb. 1798, *FBB*, p. 152.

[44] Bear, *Jefferson at Monticello*, pp. 97-99. Bacon names Jame Hubbard as the repentant thief. This is unlikely, however, as Bacon remembered that "he was always a good servant afterwards," whereas Hubbard was a chronic runaway throughout Bacon's tenure as overseer. His brother Phil is a more likely candidate for this incident.

[45] TJ to James Dinsmore, 1 Dec. 1802, DLC; TJ to Thomas Mann Randolph, 23 Jan. 1801, DLC.

[46] TJ to John Strode, 5 June 1805, DLC. The anonymous note in Jefferson's papers reporting the flogging of a slave woman, printed in Jack McLaughlin, *Jefferson and Monticello* (New York, 1988), p. 97, should be assessed with great caution. Jean Gaulmier, in *L'Idéalogue Volney*, gives the erroneous impression that Jefferson was the farmer Volney observed encouraging the pea-planting of his slaves with an almost comic frenzy of whipping (p. 370). This man was actually a French settler elsewhere in Virginia. I am grateful to C. M. Harris, editor of the William Thornton papers, for sharing his knowledge of Volney's manuscript journal, now in a private collection.

[47] Bear, *Jefferson at Monticello*, p. 97; TJ to Jeremiah Goodman, 26 July 1813, 6 Jan. 1815, *FBB*, p. 36, *GB*, p. 540. Nineteen-year-old Hercules's escapade was only the beginning of a life of resistance. He was involved in a poisoning case in 1819 and the assault on an overseer in 1822, after which he was sold (Joel Yancey to TJ, 1 July 1819, *FBB*, p. 44; TJ to Charles Clay, 9 Aug. 1819, typescript in ViU; McLaughlin, *Jefferson and Monticello*, pp. 117-18).

[48] TJ to Jeremiah Goodman, 26 July 1813, *FBB*, p. 36; TJ to John Gorman, 18 Feb. 1822, *FBB*, p. 46. Most examples are from Poplar Forest, but some of the same behavior may be assumed for Monticello, where no letters had to be written to restore harmony.

[49] I use the term "Monticello plantation" to encompass Jefferson's entire 5,000-acre operation in Albemarle County. It included the farms of Monticello and Tufton south of the Rivanna River and Shadwell and Lego on the north side.

[50] Thomas Mann Randolph to TJ, 26 Feb. 1798, ViU; John Wayles Eppes to TJ, 10 Feb. 1803, ViU; TJ to James Madison, 16 Aug. 1810, DLC; MB 25 Dec. 1809, 17 Nov. 1811; James Oldham to TJ, 26 Nov. 1804, MHi; TJ to Thomas Mann Randolph, 5 June 1805, *FBB*, p. 153. Young James Hemings ran away because of Lilly's treatment (Oldham to TJ, 16 July 1805, MHi). For other harsh overseers, see TJ to Thomas Mann Randolph, 24 June 1793, DLC; TJ to Joel Yancey, 17 Jan. 1819, *FBB*, p. 43.

[51] TJ to Reuben Perry, 16 Apr. 1812, *FBB*, p. 35. Jefferson's grandson Thomas Jefferson Randolph continued this practice. One incident stuck fast in the memory of Randolph's six-year old nephew, after a visit to Edgehill from his home in Boston. His uncle brought a slave guilty of a theft "before the house, in front of which all the slaves were assembled, and flogged him with a horsewhip" (*T. Jefferson Coolidge 1831-1920: An Autobiography*, Boston, 1923, p. 3)

[52] Bear, *Jefferson at Monticello*, p. 97.

[53] TJ to Thomas Mann Randolph, 8 June 1803, *FBB*, p. 19. Jefferson's belief in the power of positive and negative example is apparent throughout his writings. He invoked example's "terror" at least twice more in this period. In 1803 he thought a convicted slave trader should serve his term "as a terror to others." In 1809 he fervently hoped that a slave who had plundered his baggage on its way up the James River should be hanged: "Some such example is much wanting to render property waterborne secure" (TJ to Christopher Ellery, 19 May 1803, *Ford*, 9:467; TJ to John Barnes, 3 Aug. 1809, DLC). I am indebted for these citations to Philip J. Schwarz, who generously shared his "Thomas Jefferson and Slavery: A Calendar of Manuscripts and Other Primary Sources."

[54] TJ to John McDowell, 22 Oct. 1798, *FBB*, p. 437; TJ to Reuben Perry, 10 May 1811, Swem Library, College of William and Mary.

[55] Thomas Mann Randolph to TJ, 6 Mch. 1802, MHi; TJ to Randolph, 19 Apr. 1792, *Boyd*, 23:436, and 18 Feb. 1793, *FBB*, p. 165.

[56] TJ to Stevens Thomas Mason, 27 Oct. 1799, *Ford*, 9:85; TJ to William Strickland, 23 Mch. 1798, DLC.

[57] TJ to Joseph Dougherty, 31 July 1806, *FBB*, p. 22.

58 Bear, *Jefferson at Monticello*, p. 104. John Freeman and Jack Shorter, footman and groom at the President's House, had accompanied Jefferson to Monticello (see MB 20 and 21 Sep. 1806).

59 Edy was at the President's House from at least the fall of 1802 until the spring of 1809. She bore three children in that period: an infant that did not survive in Jan. 1803; James, born Jan. 1805; and Maria, born Oct. 1807 (MB 28 Jan. 1803; *FB*, p. 128). Edy, who was only fifteen when she went to Washington, may have been considered too young by her parents for formal marriage. There seems to be no way of knowing whether Jefferson gave her the option of remaining at Monticello with Joe Fossett and her family, was ignorant of the depth of her connection, or knew it and chose to disregard it.

60 This section title is drawn from Isaac Jefferson's reminiscences, Bear, *Jefferson at Monticello*, p. 19.

61 For stories told by descendants of Joe Fossett and his relatives, see Lucy C. Williams to Pearl Graham, 14 July 1947, c22 Jan. 1948; Charles H. Bullock account of Peter Fossett, cOct. 1949, Howard University Archives, Washington, DC (hereafter DHU). The silver under the portico story was also told by the Jefferson-Randolph family; butler Martin Hemings fended off the British search while Caesar shared the dark space with the silver for eighteen hours (Henry S. Randall, *The Life of Thomas Jefferson*, Philadelphia, 1865, 1.338-9). Isaac Jefferson told another story of silver saved by his father, when Benedict Arnold's forces invaded Richmond earlier in the year (Bear, *Jefferson at Monticello*, p. 8).

62 Bear, *Jefferson at Monticello*, pp. 13-14; Martha J. Randolph recollections, undated, *Boyd*, 16:168.

63 See, for instance, TJ to John McDowell, 22 Oct. 1798, *FBB*, p. 437; to John Hartwell Cocke, 3 May 1819, ViU; to James Madison, 11 Apr. 1820, *FBB*, p. 420; to John W. Eppes, 13 Oct. 1820, The Huntington Library, San Marino, CA (hereafter CSmH).

64 Brodie, *Jefferson*, p. 477; TJ to Thomas Mann Randolph, 4 Feb. 1800, DLC.

65 TJ to J. N. Demeunier, 26 June 1786, *Boyd*, 10:63; TJ to Thomas Cooper, 10 Sep. 1814, *L&B*, 14:183; "Memorandums on a Tour from Paris to Amsterdam," 19 Apr. 1788, *Boyd*, 13:36, note 29; TJ to Thomas Mann Randolph, 28 July 1793, *GB*, p. 200; Richard Beale Davis, ed., *Jeffersonian America* (1954, repr. Westport, CT, 1980), p. 149; Peden, *Notes*, pp. 139, 143.

66 TJ to Nicholas Lewis, 29 July 1787, *Boyd*, 11:640; TJ to Samuel Biddle, 12 Dec. 1792, *Boyd*, 24:725; TJ to Edward Bancroft, 26 Jan. 1789, *Boyd*, 14:492; TJ to Thomas Mann Randolph, 19 Apr. 1792, *Boyd*, 23:436.

67 [Margaret Bayard Smith], *The First Forty Years of Washington Society*, ed. Gaillard Hunt (New York, 1906), p. 68; *FBB*, p. 6; memorandums to Jeremiah Goodman, 13 Dec. 1812 and 11 Nov. 1814, *GB*, p. 493, and Princeton University Library.

68 TJ to Jeremiah Goodman, 6 Jan. 1815, *GB*, p. 539; *FB*, pp. 152,165,167.

69 Charlottesville *Daily Progress*, 25 May 1900; George Ticknor, *Life, Letters and Journals* (Boston, 1876) 1: 36; Charles M. Wiltse and Harold D. Moser, eds., *The Papers of Daniel Webster* (Hanover, NH, 1974) 1: 371.

[70] MB 13 Apr. 1811, 24 Dec. 1822, 10/11 Oct. 1823, 12 Feb. 1824; *FB*, pp. 116, 152; Edmund Bacon to TJ, 9 Sep. 1822, MHi.

[71] Record of Cases Tried in Virginia Courts, 1768-1769, DLC; Mary Rawlings, ed., *Early Charlottesville: Recollections of James Alexander 1828-1874* (Charlottesville, 1963), p. 2. Jefferson's early legal notebook was later used for Monticello household accounts by his wife Martha (1772-1782) and granddaughter Anne Cary Randolph (1805-1808). In the three years of the latter's records, every adult slave (except Sally Hemings and the two cooks) sold chickens or eggs to the Jefferson household; more than half the adults sold garden produce.

[72] MB 24 May 1795, 2 Dec. 1797, 20 Jan., 28 Oct. 1818; Nicholas Lewis accounts, 19 Sep., 28 Nov., 9 Dec. 1790, Ledger 1767-1770, ViU; Record of Cases, DLC; Lucia Goodwin, "Two Monticello Childhoods," *Anniversary Dinner at Monticello*, (Monticello, 1976), pp. 2-3.

[73] Peden, *Notes*, p. 139; TJ to Richard Richardson, 10 Feb. 1800, private collection; Bear, *Jefferson at Monticello*, p. 22.

[74] Eliza Trist to Nicholas P. Trist, 30 June 1819, DLC: Trist Papers; [Mary J. Randolph?] to Virginia J. Randolph and Jane Nicholas Randolph, 1819-1820, NcU; Bear, *Jefferson at Monticello*, p. 4; Justus, *Down from the Mountain*, p. 89; Mary J. Randolph to Virginia Randolph, 27 Dec. 1821, NcU.

[75] Martha Jefferson to TJ, 3 May 1787, *Boyd*, 11:334; Martha Randolph to Benjamin F. Randolph, 27 Jan. [1836?], ViU. Eugène Vail published six songs and two stories he heard from Martha Randolph in French in *De La Littérature et des hommes de lettres des Etats Unis d'Amérique* (Paris, 1841), pp. 321-33. I am grateful to Mechal Sobel for providing copies of the relevant pages of this rare text. Elizabeth Langhorne provided commentary and translations back into English in "Black Music and Tales from Jefferson's Monticello," *Journal of the Virginia Folklore Society* 1 (1979): 60-67. See also Mechal Sobel, *The World They Made Together: Black and White Values in Eighteenth-Century Virginia* (Princeton, 1987), pp. 141-42.

[76] Brodie, *Jefferson*, p. 474; Charlottesville *Daily Progress*, 25 May 1900; New York *World*, 30 Jan. 1898; Ellen Randolph to Virginia Randolph, 31 Aug. 1819, ViU; Robert Pleasants to TJ, 1 June 1796, William L. Clements Library, University of Michigan, and 8 Feb. 1797, Missouri Historical Society; Peden, *Notes*, p. 137; TJ to Jared Sparks, 4 Feb. 1824, *LofA*, p. 1487.

[77] TJ to Edward Bancroft, 26 Jan. 1789, *Boyd*, 14:492-93; Davis, *Jeffersonian America*, p. 149; instructions to Edmund Bacon, cOct. 1806, Bear, *Jefferson at Monticello*, p. 54.

[78] Israel Jefferson reminiscences, Brodie, *Jefferson*, p. 481; TJ-John Hemings correspondence, MHi; kitchen inventory, 20 Feb. 1796, MHi; Hannah to TJ, 15 Nov. 1818, MHi (there is a possibility this letter was written by an amanuensis); TJ to Thomas Mann Randolph, 25 Jan. and 8 Mch. 1798, *FBB*, pp. 160,243; Albemarle County Deed Book, 29:492, 36:122.

[79] There is one ambiguous payment in the 1806 Memorandum Book, to Benjamin Snead "for 2 1/2 mo[nth]s tuition of George's son" (MB 24 Sep. 1806). Isaac Jefferson's brother

George (1759-1799), a blacksmith, was always listed alone in Jefferson's Farm Book. His wife was probably either a free woman or a slave on a nearby plantation. Snead was a teacher at the neighborhood school attended by Jefferson's grandson and, if he was the same Benjamin Snead with whom Jefferson had dealings in the 1760s, he was also a weaver (Martha J. Randolph to TJ, 12 May 1798, Betts and Bear, *Family Letters*, p. 161; MB 2 Oct. 1769).

[80] TJ to James Pemberton, 21 June 1808, DLC.

[81] Mary J. Randolph to Ellen Coolidge, 11 Sep. 1825, ViU; Cornelia Randolph to Ellen Coolidge, 30 May 1830, ViU. For "poisons" and "poisoners" see, for instance, Thomas Mann Randolph to TJ, recd. 25 Apr. 1800, ViU, and Joel Yancey to TJ, 1 July 1819, *FBB*, p. 44.

[82] Auguste Levasseur, *Lafayette in America, in 1824 and 1825* (New York, 1829), p. 218. Fossett did pass on at least one overheard conversation to overseer Edmund Bacon (Bear, *Jefferson at Monticello*, p. 117.

[83] Mary J. Randolph to Ellen Coolidge, 25 Jan. 1827, ViU; Monticello dispersal sale receipts, ViU: 5921.

[84] TJ to Joseph Dougherty, 31 July 1806, *FBB*, p. 23; *Acts Passed at a General Assembly of the Commonwealth of Virginia* (Richmond, 1827), p. 127; Justus, *Down From the Mountain*, p. 121; Albemarle County Deed Book, 29: 491-92. The shop on Lot 30 on Main Street was reserved in this deed, but was probably purchased from its owner, Opie Norris, in a separate unrecorded transaction. Fossett bought the lot for $325 and sold it for $500 in 1844 (Deed Book, 42: 9-10).

[85] Albemarle County Deed Book 4: 59, 62-69; 35: 219-20; William L. Norford, *Marriages of Albemarle County and Charlottesville, 1781-1929* (Charlottesville, 1956), p. 181. Since John Winn sued Jesse Scott and the Bells for a debt, they may have bought Betsy Ann from him (Deed Book, 29:442; 36: 121-22).

[86] See Charlottesville Deed Book, 3: 270 for sale of the building out of the family 15 July 1892. Another probable link between Monticello and Charlottesville is Daniel Farley, whose house in the town may have been a Sunday gathering spot for Jefferson's slaves. In 1816 Moses broke his leg "in a trial of strength in a wrestle with one of his fellows" and was "at Farley's" (Frank Carr to TJ, 18 Mch. 1816, *FBB*, p. 40). County records, which need further study, suggest that Farley is Mary Hemings's son, and Joe Fossett's brother, Daniel (b. 1772), given in the 1780s to Jefferson's sister Anna (*FB*, p. 24; "Negroes Alienated"; Albemarle County Will Book, 13: 44; Deed Book 36: 27-28).

[87] Orra Langhorne, *Southern Sketches from Virginia 1881-1901*, ed. Charles E. Wynes (Charlottesville, 1964), pp. 81-83. Sally and Jesse Scott's children did, in fact, attend the white school in Charlottesville. This work and a number of other sources on the Scotts were kindly brought to my attention by the staff of the Albemarle County Historical Society. Olivia Summers Dutcher deserves credit for sparking my interest in Jesse Scott and the resultant discovery of his connection with the Hemingses of Monticello. She is the owner of a delightful oil portrait of Scott with his violin, and she and her late husband assembled a great deal of information on the musician and his instrument.

[88] Charlottesville *Daily Progress*, 25 May 1900; Justus, *Down from the Mountain*, p. 122-24; Charles H. Bullock account of Peter Fossett, cOct. 1949, DHU.

[89] Justus, *Down from the Mountain*, pp. 122-24; Fossett obituary, Cincinnati newspaper, 1901, Monticello archives.

THE
FOSSETT
FAMILY

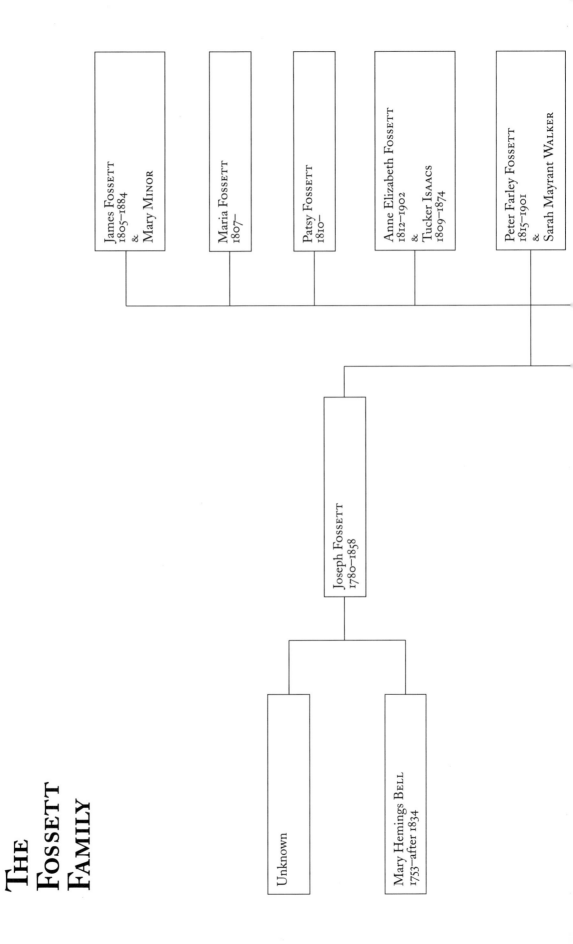

James Fossett
1805–1884
&
Mary Minor

Maria Fossett
1807–

Patsy Fossett
1810–

Anne Elizabeth Fossett
1812–1902
&
Tucker Isaacs
1809–1874

Peter Farley Fossett
1815–1901
&
Sarah Mayrant Walker

Joseph Fossett
1780–1858

Unknown

Mary Hemings Bell
1753–after 1834

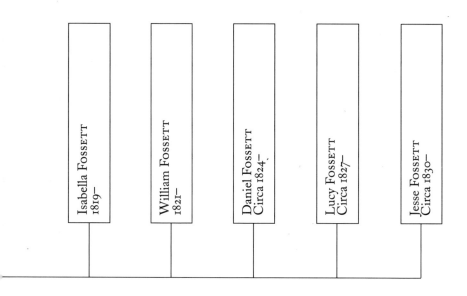

Isabella Fossett
1819–

William Fossett
1821–

Daniel Fossett
Circa 1824–

Lucy Fossett
Circa 1827–

Jesse Fossett
Circa 1830–

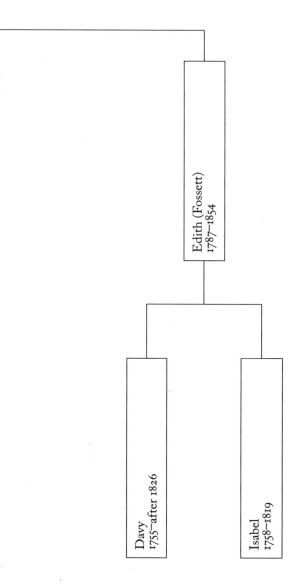

Edith (Fossett)
1787–1854

Davy
1755–after 1826

Isabel
1758–1819